"One of the most important contributions to the study of American history that I have ever experienced."
—Henry Louis Gates Jr., director of the W.E.B. Du Bois Institute for African American Research

"This was a horrific time in our history, but it needs to be taught and seen and heard. This is very well done, very well done."
—Malaak Shabazz, daughter of Malcolm X and Betty Shabazz, on the Jim Crow Museum

"The [Jim Crow Museum's] contents are only a small part of the damaging effects of the Jim Crow laws that were found all across America, including bright and sunny California. This history is not only an important part of understanding where America was but, in an age of states making it harder and harder for citizens to vote, it is relevant to note that we have been here before."
—Henry Rollins, host of the History Channel's *10 Things You Don't Know About*

"For decades the author has been on a Pilgrimage to bring out from our dank closets the racial skeletons of our past. His is a crucial mission, because he forces us to realize that race relations grew worse in the first several decades of the twentieth century— something many Americans never knew or now want to suppress. This book allows us to see, even feel, the racism of just a generation or two ago—and Pilgrim shows that elements of it continue, even today. See it! Read it! Feel it! Then help us all transcend it!"
—James W. Loewen, author of *Lies My Teacher Told Me* and coeditor of *The Confederate and Neo-Confederate Reader*

"The [Jim Crow Museum] has been one of my treasured go-to resources for teaching people about the deep-seated roots of the racism that persists in our collective subconscious. Only by facing our history and its hold on our psyche can we construct a better culture. This work is invaluable."
—damali ayo, author of *How to Rent a Negro* and *Obamistan! Land wi*

D0838746

Haste to Rise
A Remarkable Experience of Black Education during Jim Crow

David Pilgrim and Franklin Hughes

Haste to Rise: A Remarkable Experience of Black Education during Jim Crow
David Pilgrim and Franklin Hughes
© 2020 PM Press

ISBN: 978-1-62963-790-7 (print)
ISBN: 978-1-62963-814-0 (ebook)
Library of Congress Control Number: 2019946091

Cover by John Yates / www.stealworks.com
Interior design by briandesign

10 9 8 7 6 5 4 3 2 1

PM Press
PO Box 23912
Oakland, CA 94623
www.pmpress.org

Printed in the USA

We dedicate this book to Samantha Bahl. Fly on, little wing.

God of the morning, at whose voice
The cheerful sun makes haste to rise,
And like a giant doth rejoice
To run his journey through the skies.

—Isaac Watts

Bruno Chenu, *The Trouble I've Seen: The Big Book of Negro Spirituals* (Valley Forge, PA: Judson Press, 2003), 90.

Contents

—

Foreword

David Eisler

The road to discovery often begins with a single step. What started as a small project to locate a photo of the first African American student at Ferris Institute became something that could not have been anticipated. When David Pilgrim and Franklin Hughes began uncovering information about our founder Woodbridge Nathan Ferris and his extraordinary efforts to welcome all students to his institute, it brought a heightened sense of purpose and meaning to our university. This was a history we had lost, a part of our heritage unknown to us until now. It was exciting to watch and learn as their research revealed first one and then another and another of the successful graduates who journeyed north from the Hampton Institute to the Ferris Institute. These discoveries are stories meant to be shared, documenting the legacy we are entrusted to continue.

The day David approached me about writing the foreword for this book, it required little discussion. If my memory serves, it may have been one of the shortest conversations we have ever had. The discovery about our founders and the open arms they extended to the young African American men who came to the institute in the early 1900s is an extraordinary story and needs to be told.

When Mr. Ferris was searching for a place to establish a school, he had three locations in mind—Fargo, North Dakota, Duluth, Minnesota, and Big Rapids, Michigan. He ultimately chose Big Rapids, because there was not a school like what he envisioned within a fifty-mile radius. His intent, when he and his wife Helen established our school in 1884, was to build a school for lumberjacks, miners, farmers' sons and daughters, and girls who worked in Michigan factories. They set out to change the lives of men and women who did not have access to the education they deserved. They wanted better lives not only for them but also for their families.

The initial class of fifteen students, composed of both men and women, was an early indication of the type of learning institution Mr. and Mrs. Ferris would establish. It would be, above everything else, a place of opportunity and access to education for all. These tenets, deeply ingrained into the foundation of this institution, continue to be a driving force in all we do for our students.

Mr. Ferris said that the education he received as a young boy was "the horror of his life." Thanks to his mother he did learn to read, and by the time he was ten years old, he was reading news about the Civil War to his father, who could not read or write and was slightly deaf. In this, he learned to speak very clearly, which would undoubtedly help him later in life as a teacher, businessman, public speaker, and elected official.

Throughout his life, Woodbridge N. Ferris believed it was his calling to serve others, to build up women and men, to help them rise, and to instill in them an appreciation for the fundamental values of life. While teaching and operating Ferris Institute, he made it a practice every morning to gather the student body for "morning exercises." These included singing, reading the works of great leaders, and listening to short talks meant to provide daily inspiration. He made every effort to inspire his students to a realization of their possibilities. He was once quoted as saying, "I have always entertained the notion that the majority of mankind sleep twenty-four hours a day. Awaken students to a realization of what it means to live and they will have little difficulty in performance." He was a firm believer in helping people achieve something greater.

While much is known and continues to be discovered about Mr. Ferris, less is written about Mrs. Ferris. From the beginning, she played a pivotal role alongside him. She taught with Mr. Ferris for the first seventeen years of the institute, before illness forced her retirement, and, as Mr. Ferris once said, "She was eager to encourage and instruct the most backward and discouraged."

Mrs. Ferris spent much time teaching and assisting Mr. Ferris with affairs at the institute, but she also took great care and time with their home and children and the school's students. Until 1911, she kept their home open to students. Some went there for homework help. Others came to borrow books. She spent her Sunday evenings reading the likes of "Wild Animals I Have Known," "Cudjo's Cave," "Modern Vikings," and

Woodbridge Ferris (second row, far left) and Helen Ferris (second row, far right) are pictured with students in 1888, four years after the founding of their school.

other tales, with up to sixteen students in attendance some evenings. She enjoyed teaching, and students thought fondly of her.

Helen supported Woodbridge in many of his endeavors and was likely the most ardent supporter of his political activities, all the while knowing he had not a political bone in his body. As a two-time governor and a senator of Michigan, Woodbridge said Helen was a major contributing factor to his success. Her life, he once said, illuminated his pathway. After her passing, when confronted with problems, he would ask himself, "What would Mrs. Ferris suggest or advise, if she were at my side?"

Mr. and Mrs. Ferris were truly American originals, educational pioneers. Mr. Ferris had the ability to discern truth, to firmly recognize right and wrong, and to live his life serving others, no matter the color of their skin, their age, sex, or status. Mrs. Ferris was equally steeped in and guided by virtue. They had a clear and shared vision of what the Ferris Institute was and could and should be. Their vision of embracing those who wanted to learn and preparing them for the opportunity of success in their chosen careers are precepts we deeply value to this day. We remain an institution committed to building an inclusive university—in Woodbridge's words, "a school for all people regardless of race or station."

In reading and reflecting on this book, I challenge you to consider how we take the example of Woodbridge and Helen Ferris and apply it today, providing educational opportunity and access for all. And as we look to the future, each of us should be emboldened to further the vision Woodbridge and Helen Ferris advanced 135 years ago—a vision that goes above and beyond for our students, for our state and all of humankind, for today, now, and always.

The painting *The Visionary* (center panel) is located in the Arts and Sciences Building at Ferris State University.

The uneducated Negro is a good Negro; he is contented to occupy the natural status of his race, the position of inferiority. The educated Negro, who wants to vote, is a disturbing and threatening influence. We don't want him down here; let him go North.

—Hoke Smith, U.S. senator, Georgia

"Intelligent Negro Disturbing Influence," *Appeal* (Saint Paul, MN), November 4, 1916, 1.

—

First Words

by David Pilgrim

A mural troubles me.

It is not a mural in the narrow sense—a painting on a wall; rather, it is a free-hanging oil painting on a stretched canvas. The mural is a massive triptych displayed in the atrium of the Arts and Sciences building at Ferris State University. The three panels are presented in an inverted T shape. The left panel, *Movers and Shakers*, portrays President Bill Sederburg and his administrative team as they plan the university's future. The right panel, *Activities*, is a collection of fictional student athletes. The center panel is called *The Visionary*. The dominant figure is Woodbridge Nathan Ferris, the university's founder. He is larger than the other figures and appears to be looking over them as they continue the work that he began in 1884.

The mural is a visual success. This is not surprising. Robert Barnum, the mural's creator, is an award-winning artist. His skill as an artist and his familiarity with the institution—he had been employed as a professor for seven years—made him a likely candidate for painting the mural. Barnum envisioned it as "the historical, allegorical painting of Ferris State University," and he used his paintbrushes to tell the story that he knew.[1]

The story that Barnum knew—indeed, the story that most of us knew—had little to say about the African American presence at Ferris State University. Although there are a couple of racially ambiguous characters in the painting, there is only one figure who clearly represents an African American: a black man holding a sign—"Negotiate Now!"—supporting the faculty union in a dispute against the institution's administration.[2]

Viewers of the mural might reasonably infer that African Americans were of little consequence in the history of the university.

For seventeen years I taught sociology at Ferris State University; for much of that time, I had an office in the Arts and Sciences building, so I saw that mural hundreds of times. My critique of the painting is softened by the realization that even though I am an African American—one who frequently taught courses about race relations—I too knew little about the history of African Americans at Ferris. I had heard stories about racial fights in the 1960s and student protests in the 1980s, and I had a vague knowledge of Gideon Smith, reputed to have been the first African American student at Ferris. That was all I knew. It pains me to say this, but the mural bothered me, because I believed it was true, a historically accurate interpretation of the past.

Now, I know better.

In 2007, I left the classroom to become the university's first chief diversity officer, a position that morphed into the role of vice president for diversity and inclusion. Although I missed my students, I welcomed the opportunity to help transform the institution into a more diverse and inclusive university. For a year, the university engaged in productive—sometimes difficult—discussions about its future. We emerged from that year with our first diversity plan, one based on the belief that Ferris State University is at its best when all its members believe that the university belongs to them as much as it belongs to anyone.

I remained troubled by the mural.

More accurately, the many murals, paintings, and sculptures on the campus troubled me, because they rarely included representations of people of color. The art that a community produces and displays gives essential clues about that community's attitudes, tastes, and values—and, equally significant, the art tells us what the community believes is important in its past and present. By 2015, Ferris State University had adopted diversity as one of its core values, had almost doubled the number of students of color, and was actively trying to recruit a more diverse faculty and staff.[3] The time seemed right to add to the university's public art. I planned to start by commissioning a painting of Gideon Smith.

I asked Franklin Hughes, a multimedia specialist and researcher in the Diversity and Inclusion Office, to find photographs of Smith. The plan was to give the pictures to Diane Cleland, a local artist—and a docent in the Jim Crow Museum—so she could use them to paint a portrait of Smith.

Hughes's research took him to a time before Ferris was a university, before it was a college, back to its early years as an institute. He soon discovered that Smith was not the first African American student at Ferris.

In the first decade of the twentieth century, there was a student enrolled in the pharmacy program at Ferris Institute who is described in various documents as *mulatto, colored,* or *black*. His name was Middleton E. Pickens. He was born in 1875 in Winnsborough, South Carolina.[4] Pickens attended Lincoln University in Pennsylvania from 1892 to 1897, earning a college preparatory degree and a general collegiate degree. He arrived in Big Rapids around 1900 and found work as a hotel porter. That year, Pickens enrolled in the Ferris Institute to study pharmacy. He was the editor of the "Pharmacy Department" column in the *Ferris Institute News*. In January 1902, he was one of nine applicants to receive an Assistant Pharmacist Certificate from the Michigan Board of Pharmacy.[5] Later, Pickens received a Doctor of Medicine degree from the Detroit College of Medicine.

While in Detroit, Pickens became active in politics. In 1904, he was a member of the Colored Voters Independent Club and president of the Colored Men's Ferris Club, a group of African American registered voters who supported Woodbridge Ferris's first bid to become governor of the state.[6] By 1909, Pickens had moved to Oklahoma. In that year, he was elected as vice president of the Young Men's Republican Club in Muskogee. He would later serve as president of the Independent Colored Voters Club.[7] Pickens practiced medicine (and politics) in Muskogee until his death on December 30, 1915.[8] He was a respected community leader; this is evident in an obituary that appeared in a Tulsa newspaper:[9]

> That "death loves a shining mark" was forcibly brought to the attention of the minds and hearts of many Muskogeans last Thursday by the unexpected taking off of that well known and popular Negro physician, Dr. M.E. Pickens, just as he was passing from young manhood to cross the threshold of middle age. It would be difficult for one to name a man professionally engaged as he was more widely admired and beloved, and this is because his medical attainments were above question and criticism and also that he was a man of proverbial generous and good nature. His sad decrease was not alone a shock to the immediate family but to the community.[10]

Woodbridge Ferris made personal loans to Pickens totaling $845 over four years—a period that corresponded with Pickens's time at the Detroit

College of Medicine. It is noteworthy that a white college president made a substantial loan—in 2020 dollars, the debt plus the four-year interest would be almost $20,000—to a former student, a "colored" student, to attend medical school. The more we researched the life and work of Woodbridge Ferris, the clearer it became that he helped many students. According to one newspaper:

> Nobody ever had to worry about the wherewithal for tuition fees at Ferris Institute, which specialized in training pharmacists. If young men or women looked promising, Ferris had a habit of letting them give notes for their college expenses and redeem them any time in the future when they were in business for themselves and could pay them without difficulty. In his private safe at Big Rapids, Ferris always had on hand a stack of promissory notes from former students, and was fond of telling that mighty few of them ever went to protest.[11]

Pickens died before he repaid the loan.

In 1902, Nathan "Nate" Harris, another "colored" student, enrolled at Ferris Institute. Harris's life is chronicled—or at least mentioned—in several history books, especially ones that examine Negro League baseball. According to the U.S. Census, Nathan was born in Middleport, Ohio, in 1880. His mother, Rosa Harris, a black woman, was a cook on a steamboat. Nate is listed as a mulatto.[12] Little is known of his father. If he was white, it is a safe assumption that the couple did not marry; interracial marriages were illegal in Ohio when Nathan was born.[13] Rosa later married Samuel Washington, a black man. The family moved to Columbus, Ohio, when Nate was fourteen years old. After a few years, they moved to Pittsburgh, Pennsylvania.

Harris was a superior athlete, excelling in baseball and football. He began a semi-professional baseball career as a third baseman in 1898 with the Pittsburgh Keystones, a famed all-black team. He sustained a football injury in 1899 and, therefore, did not play baseball or football that year. In 1900, his injuries healed, he pitched and played third base for the Smoky City Giants, another all-black team in Pittsburgh. John W. "Bud" Fowler, the first African American to play professional baseball—meaning, the white major and minor leagues—owned and played on the team. Fowler played in the 1870s and 1880s, before the Major Leagues drew the color line that banned black players until Jackie Robinson joined the Brooklyn Dodgers in 1947.[14]

Nate Harris (second row, far left) is shown with the 1909 Leland Giants.

In 1901, Harris played for the Chicago Columbia Giants. That year, the team merged with the Chicago Union to become the Chicago Union Giants. Frank Leland, one of the early and most prominent leaders of Negro League baseball, owned the Giants. The following year, during a barnstorming tour of Michigan, they played a two-game series against a Big Rapids team. The Chicago Union Giants must have liked Big Rapids, because a little more than a month later the team moved there. Initially, the plan was to merge the all-black Chicago Union Giants with the all-white Big Rapids Giants. The prospects of the two teams merging excited the local Big Rapids community:

> The hiring of the colored players means that baseball enthusiasm
> has revived in this city, and that our people are to witness some
> hot games during the balance of the season. It also means that Big
> Rapids is now prepared to play ball with any team in the country,
> and that some first-class teams will be seen here in the near future.[15]

It was only nominally a merger. Shortly after arriving, the Big Rapids baseball team became—in name and practice—the Colored Giants. The team played and won against first-class competition, including a two-game set against future hall of famer Andrew "Rube" Foster and the Otsego (Michigan) Independents.[16] The Big Rapids team had great players, including Charlie Grant, John Davis, Grant "Homerun" Johnson, William

Buckner, Joe Green, and Nate Harris. Leland was not a part of the new team. Instead, he remained in Chicago and rebuilt the Chicago Union squad with players from other black teams. In August 1902, the Big Rapids Giants defeated Leland's Chicago Union team to win what was billed as the Colored Championship of the World.[17] Harris was a star in the clinching game. He had three hits in five at-bats and scored three runs. Despite its success, the baseball team did not remain in Big Rapids. After only one season, the team disbanded, with players going to other squads. In 1903, Harris played for the Cuban Giants (Cuban X Giants) of New York.

By 1905, Harris had once again become one of Leland's players. The Chicago Union Giants—now called the Leland Giants—had quickly become the best all-black team in the Midwest. The Giants won 122 games, lost only ten, and compiled an incredible forty-eight-game winning streak. The Leland Giants were popular, often drawing more than five thousand spectators to their games, a large number of paying customers for a game starring black players in the early 1900s.

Harris had short-lived (sometimes very short) playing stints with other teams, including the Philadelphia Giants, where, in 1906, he was again a member of a Colored World Championship team.[18] However, he spent much of the remainder of his career playing with the Leland Giants. One of his career highlights and a highpoint for the Giants occurred in 1909. The Leland Giants played the all-white Chicago Cubs in a three-game series. Although the Giants lost all three games—two by a single run—they were competitive against a Major League team that won 104 games in the National League.[19]

In 1910, the Leland Giants, with Harris as captain and manager, loaded their bats and gloves onto buses and into motorcars and embarked on a barnstorming trip to play the "leading college teams and crack teams of the large Southern cities."[20] When they traveled through Virginia, they stopped to play the Hampton Institute Baseball Cubs. Later that year, Gideon Smith enrolled at the Ferris Institute in the College Preparatory Department. There is no evidence that Nate Harris met Gideon Smith while in Hampton, Virginia, but he may have.

Nate Harris is included in most histories of Negro League baseball. And that is as it should be. He excelled on many of the best teams between 1900 and 1910. He was a slick fielding infielder and a solid contact hitter. He was best known for his speed, often leading his team in steals and runs scored. Although he does not get the credit, Harris performed a hook slide two years before Ty Cobb was celebrated for his famous "fade away slide."[21] Sportswriter and fellow player Jimmy Smith put Harris on his 1909 "All American Team."[22] In 1952, Harris received votes in a *Pittsburgh Courier* poll to identify the best players in the Negro Leagues.

When his playing days were over, he coached, mentored, and instructed younger players. In 1925, the *Pittsburgh Courier* reported on Harris's work with the Homestead Grays, one of the premier teams in the Negro Leagues.[23] The article succinctly assessed Harris's career:

> Nate Harris, prominent Hill business man and affectionately known as the "daddy" of baseball in this district, is taking charge of the daily workouts of the Homestead Grays. Nate was in charge last week at Washington Park, and put the lads through some snappy practice sessions. Nate, for many years, ranked as the premier Negro second-baseman of this country, playing for years with Rube Foster and his club.[24]

Football was Harris's other athletic passion. After the 1902 baseball season, he remained in Big Rapids to coach and play football for the Ferris Institute. He excelled on the playing field.[25] In a game against Traverse City, framed as the "championship of northern and western Michigan in football outside of the college teams," Harris performed so well that he was carried off the field on the shoulders of Ferris students, including teammates—*at halftime*. The Ferris Institute football team won the game and finished the season with a 5–2–1 record. *The Big Rapids Pioneer* applauded him:

> The features of the game were end runs of Harris and his beautiful drop kick from the thirty yard line. The development of the team under his coaching is noticed, as they seem to know the game better and play it better than ever before.[26]

There was a great deal of excitement for the 1903 football season. Woodbridge Ferris became a fan. His newfound interest in the sport was evident in several talks before the student body. He said, "The institution cannot get along this year without a team," and he promised to "do all in his power toward the organization and maintenance of a fast one."[27] This was a strong endorsement from a man who until that time had seen football as insignificant. More than fifty students tried out for the team, including "a large number of upper peninsula boys . . . big, strong, well-built fellows."[28] A local newspaper touted the role that Harris would play:

Nathan Harris, the colored boy who performed miracles with the pig-skin on last year's team, has been engaged as coach, and is expected in the city soon. He is the fellow who in the Ferris-Traverse City game here last Thanksgiving day, alone and without interference passed five Traverse City players, each some distance apart on the field, and scored a touch-down.[29]

Alas, the 1903 Ferris Institute football team struggled, finishing with a 1–3 record. The team lost to their Traverse City rivals, 10–0. A Traverse City newspaper wrote, "Harris, the negro coach of F.I., was in the game, but it made no difference."[30] The Ferris Institute team was competitive against Traverse City, but they had no chance against Fielding Yost's powerful University of Michigan squad. The Ferris team lost 88–0. According to a Detroit newspaper, during the game, "Harris, the colored halfback, was carted off the field on the account of an injury."[31] After 1903, Harris's focus returned to baseball, where he continued to distinguish himself as a player, then later as a manager. Few people know that Nate Harris was one of the first African Americans to coach football at a historically white institute.

The search for a photograph of Gideon Smith started us on a journey that also led to Chester E. Bush, who took business courses at Ferris Institute between 1903 and 1905. He was born on January 16, 1886, in Little Rock, Arkansas, to John E. and Cora Bush. The elder Bush was a prominent African American activist, entrepreneur, and politician. In 1883, he and Chester W. Keatts founded the Mosaic Templars of America (MTA), which became one of the most successful black-owned business enterprises in the nation.[32] The name was inspired by Moses, the biblical prophet who led the Israelites out of enslavement. The MTA began as a vehicle to help poor black people, many of them former slaves, pay for medical care and burial rites. The organization grew rapidly. By the 1920s, they had more than eighty thousand members. At its peak, it included a hospital, publishing house, business college, nursing school, and insurance company.[33] Today, a rebuilt MTA building serves as a community center.

The MTA made John Bush one of the wealthiest black men in Arkansas—and his national stature brought praise from his friend Booker T. Washington. Bush served on the executive committee of Washington's National Negro Business League, and Washington advised him on the affairs of the MTA.[34] Politicians in Washington, DC, also noticed Bush. In 1898, President McKinley appointed Bush the receiver (public money handler) for the United States Land Office in Little Rock. This was at that time the highest federal appointment of an African American west of the Mississippi. Presidents Theodore Roosevelt and William Howard Taft reappointed him.

C. E. BUSH
NATIONAL GRAND SCRIBE-TREASURER

Chester Bush was groomed to succeed his father. In 1906, both men joined Washington and a team of African American business leaders and traveled across the Southwest, preaching hard work, thrift, and home ownership.[35]

Chester E. Bush of the Mosaic Templars, 1924

Chester became manager and editor of the *Mosaic Guide*, the official publication of the MTA. In 1907, he was described as "the youngest editor of color in the United States."[36] The following year, Chester served as manager of the Arkansas Mutual Aid Association, the only health benefits and burial expenses provider for African Americans in Arkansas. In 1916, after his father's death, he was promoted to National Grand Scribe and Treasurer of the Mosaic Templars. Chester and his brother Aldridge helped establish the first local branch of the National Association for the Advancement of Colored People (NAACP) in Little Rock, Arkansas, in 1918.

Bush's role as the publisher of the *Mosaic Guide* gave him national visibility. In July 1918, he was part of a contingent invited to the White House to strategize the role of African Americans in World War I. The assembly included W.E.B. Du Bois, Robert L. Vann, Benjamin J. Davis, and Robert R. Moton. The group developed a resolution acknowledging the worldwide threat of Germany, while simultaneously defending the patriotism of the African American community:

> We deem it hardly necessary, in view of the untarnished record of
> Negro Americans, to reaffirm our loyalty to our country and our

readiness to make every sacrifice to win this war. . . . [W]e believe today that justifiable grievances of the Colored people are producing not disloyalty, but an amount of unrest and bitterness. . . . German propaganda among us is powerless, but the apparent indifference of our own government may be dangerous. . . . The American Negro . . . is more than willing to share in helping win the war for democracy and he expects his full share of the fruits thereof.[37]

Chester Bush died at the relatively young age of thirty-eight. In his short life, he extended the work that he inherited from his father: building and sustaining a business enterprise that catered to the needs of black people—and advocating for the interests of black people.

We identified a fourth African American who attended Ferris Institute before Gideon Smith. His name was Edgar Emmason McDaniel, and he is listed in the 1903–1905 *Catalog of Ferris Institute*. As was true with Chester Bush, McDaniel's family was well-to-do and his father a member of Booker T. Washington's National Negro Business League. In 1916, the *Topeka Plaindealer*, a black-owned newspaper, praised the elder McDaniel and his family:

> The McDaniel family is one of the foremost of the race, each member being a real doer. His long years of experience along business lines makes him the man for the position of grand chancellor. For eighteen years he has been a railroad contractor, having been employed by the leading railroads of the country. The McDaniel residence is one of the best in Oklahoma, being a two-story and a swell home indeed. Mrs. McDaniel at present is matron at Langston University and it is said that she is making one of the best the school ever had. A son, Edgar E. McDaniel, Jr., an expert bookkeeper, is secretary of the university. This young man is not only a prepared man, but an ideal fellow, one of the race's ripe scholars, being a graduate of Ferris Institute. Miss Blanche, a daughter, is a student, and Miss Hazel, another daughter, is one of the popular teachers in the Tulsa colored high school.[38]

In 1921, the *Plaindealer* described the younger McDaniel as an educated, "highly cultured" young businessman.[39] He left bookkeeping work at Langston University and took a clerk position at the Poro Beauty College in St. Louis, Missouri. It was founded by Annie Minerva Turnbo Malone as a commercial and educational enterprise centered on cosmetics for African

Frank Roberts (second row, third from the right) is pictured in the 1912 pharmacy class at Ferris Institute.

American women. She launched her hair care business four years before Sarah Breedlove (later known as Madam C.J. Walker), who worked as a "Poro Agent" for one year. By 1923, McDaniel was the office manager at Poro. He was, in the words of the *Plaindealer*, "very energetic, efficient and competent to manage such a concern."[40] McDaniel relocated to Chicago when Poro moved there in 1930 and likely worked there until his death in 1956.[41]

Middleton E. Pickens, Nate Harris, Chester Bush, and Edgar E. McDaniel were remarkable men and represent an African American presence at Ferris several years before Gideon Smith came to Big Rapids.[42] We also found a contemporary of Smith: Frank M. Roberts, an African American from St. Joseph, Michigan, one of seven students pictured in graduation garb with the pharmacy class in 1912. Roberts enrolled at Ferris in September 1910—as early as, if not earlier than, Smith. As a native of Michigan, it made sense that Roberts might attend Ferris Institute, located in Big Rapids, Michigan; but Smith was a native of Virginia. We discovered other African Americans in the first two decades of the twentieth century—all males, many from the Old Dominion state.

William Milton Howard, an African American, was pictured in the 1913 yearbook. He spent a year at Ferris Institute, and then entered the Dental School of the University of Michigan, graduating in 1917. Howard

James Duncan (first row, far left) and John Smith (second row, far left) are shown on the 1915 Ferris Institute basketball team.

entered the Medical Officers' Reserve Corps but was not called to service. He opened a dental practice in Detroit, Michigan, around 1920, likely becoming the youngest African American dentist in that city.

In the 1915 *Crimson and Gold*, there is a picture of the school's basketball team. There are six members of the team, two of them are—to use the language of today—men of color. They were James Duncan and John Swinerton Smith. It is not inconsequential that long before it was popular—or even legal in some places—the Ferris Institute basketball team was interracial. There were very few African American basketballers—one source says about nineteen—who had the opportunity to play on integrated teams before World War I.[43] It would not be until the 1940s that the Big Ten schools integrated and not until the 1960s that most major colleges had integrated basketball teams.[44]

Duncan attended Hampton Institute until 1913 and played on the basketball and football teams while attending Ferris Institute. He was enrolled in the Normal Department. Little is known of his life after leaving Ferris, other than that he served as a sergeant at Camp Funston in Kansas, in 1918, and later worked in the auto industry in Detroit. Smith was a machinist student at Hampton, graduating in 1913. He played on the Hampton

Walter Lowe, Harry Munford, and Arthur Wells (bottom, center photo, left to right) in the 1917 *Crimson and Gold* yearbook.

football team. At Ferris, he was enrolled in the Commercial Department from October 1913 to March 1915. Like Duncan, Smith played on the basketball and football teams. After Ferris, he returned to Newport News, Virginia, his hometown, and worked as a driller in a shipyard, a salesman in the industrial industry, and, in his later years, as an independent real estate broker. Smith was also the president of Pleasant Shade Cemetery Company, the first public cemetery opened for African Americans in the Hampton-Newport News area.[45]

Harry James Munford, from West Norfolk, Virginia, attended the Hampton Institute from 1913 to 1915.[46] He enrolled in the pharmacy program at Ferris in 1916. In June 1917, he was one of 109 Michigan candidates to pass the Michigan Board of Pharmacy examination.[47] He moved to Detroit to practice. Munford served in the Medical Detachment 535th Engineer Service Battalion (colored) in France during World War I.[48] After the war, he returned to Virginia and was a pharmacist in Portsmouth. By the 1930 U.S. Census, Munford was a pharmacist in Manhattan, New York. He died in New York in June 1967.

These were all young African American men who attended Hampton Institute (today, Hampton University) before coming to Ferris

Institute—and there were others. This relationship between Ferris Institute and Hampton Institute intrigued us; more specifically, we wanted to know more about the young men who bonded the two schools—and we wanted to know what became of them. This, then, became for us the bigger story.

Today, Hampton University is a major American institution—offering fifty baccalaureate programs, twenty-six master's programs, and seven doctoral programs; however, in the early 1900s, it was mainly a trade school.[49] One of the Hampton students who came to Ferris said this of the Hampton curriculum in the early 1900s:

> I have also noted the somewhat restricted academic studies at Hampton, no mathematics, beyond arithmetic, no language but English, a modest amount of physics and chemistry. This did not mean that the executives and teachers had an opinion of the limited ability of the students. They knew that studies were never going to be a part of the life and work of these students. They realized that they were not going to Harvard or Yale, but rather to the University of Hard Knocks. The feeling was that they needed only enough education to teach in primary or elementary schools, or to bolster their efficiency and understanding of the trades they were learning. They needed only enough education to establish them as school, church, or hard-work leaders in their communities when they returned.[50]

In the early 1900s, Hampton students who wanted college preparatory courses or college courses had to go to other institutions, and Jim Crow laws and customs necessitated they leave the South.[51] George Swanson was the first black student admitted to the University of Virginia—and that was in 1950. With help from the NAACP, he won a federal lawsuit that allowed him to attend the University of Virginia's law school. A few black undergraduate students were admitted to Virginia Polytechnic Institute in 1953 and the University of Virginia in 1955. However, those institutions and other white colleges in the state remained largely (and functionally) segregated until the 1960s. The Hampton students who came to Ferris did so decades before they would have been allowed to attend "white" colleges in Virginia.

Maceo Richard Clarke attended Hampton Institute from 1915 to 1918 and entered Ferris Institute in 1919,[52] where he played on the baseball team and was a noncommissioned officer in the Ferris Reserve Officers'

Maceo Clarke (back row, second from right) wore a Hampton Institute cap in a 1919 Ferris Institute baseball team picture.

Training Corps (ROTC).[53] After taking college preparatory courses, he moved on to Howard University, where he received a bachelor's degree and played on the university's baseball team. While at Howard, he was also a pitcher for the Washington Potomacs, a Negro League team.[54] As a member of the Potomacs, Clarke was a teammate of Benjamin Harris Taylor, a stellar player and manager elected to the Major League Baseball Hall of Fame in 2006.[55] Clarke eventually put away his baseball cleats and pursued medical studies at Meharry Medical College, in Nashville, Tennessee. He lived to be ninety years of age, and most of his adult life was spent practicing medicine in Ohio. In 1963, Governor James A. Rhodes appointed Clarke to the Ohio Board of Regents, the coordinating board for higher education in Ohio. The appointment of an African American to a powerful statewide board—one that advised the governor and the Ohio General Assembly—was a significant event during the civil rights era.

Maceo had two relatives who enrolled at Hampton and Ferris: an older brother, Walter, and a younger brother, Hannibal. Both men practiced dentistry, but Hannibal also distinguished himself as a civic leader in West Virginia.[56] He practiced dentistry for more than fifty years in Williamson, West Virginia. His community involvement included serving as a member of the board of commissioners of the Housing Authority of Williamson, chairperson of the board of the Mingo County Economic Opportunity Commission, director of Logan-Mingo Area Mental Health Inc., and director of the American Red Cross. In the first half of the twentieth century, it was common for African American dentists to be active in the American civil rights movement. Hannibal was a lifetime member of the NAACP, heading the Williamson chapter for eighteen years. A Marshall University publication described him as "the area leader in the early days of integration in ensuring harmony among races."[57] In 1995, Marshall University established the Dr. Hannibal D. Clarke Scholarship in his memory.

The Clarke brothers and other young African American men who left Hampton Institute to come to Ferris Institute in the early 1900s wanted to attend colleges and universities; they also wanted to escape—if only temporarily—the daily and ubiquitous indignities suffered under the Jim Crow racial hierarchy. Not coincidently, the Hampton Institute students came to Ferris Institute during a time when thousands of black people were permanently leaving the South. This mass exodus of black people, often referred to as the Great Migration, reached a peak during World War I, when seven hundred thousand to one million left the rural South to create new lives in the urban, industrial North.[58] In the 1920s, another eight hundred thousand black people left the South.[59]

Black newspapers, most notably, the *Chicago Defender*, the nation's leading black newspaper at the time, portrayed the North as a Promised Land, a land of milk and honey for a people thirsty and hungry for freedom. The Hebrews in the Old Testament fled enslavement in Egypt in search of Canaan, their Promised Land; black newspapers urged—even begged—black people to flee a slave-like status in the South and come to the North, the New Canaan. The *pull* was also economic. The widespread enlistment of soldiers left vacancies in the industrial labor force. This meant jobs for black people: jobs outside of the Jim Crow South.

The *push* factors were more numerous: denial of suffrage, corruption in local criminal justice systems, a racially segregated southern economy—including debt slavery (peonage), educational inequality at all levels, and the very real threat of physical assaults, murders, lynchings, and riots. It is not hyperbolic to say that it was dangerous to live as a black person in many parts of the South during the Jim Crow era.

Alas, the North was no Shangri-La. The migrating blacks, barred from most labor unions, worked jobs at the bottom of the economic ladder: janitors, porters, domestic and commercial cleaners, and sanitation workers.

Newspaper clippings about the 1919 race riots

Housing was racially segregated and rundown. Some black people did find and make better lives, but many others did not materially improve their circumstances—they exchanged lives in rural shacks in the South for overcrowded, disease-infected slums in Chicago, New York, Detroit, Baltimore, Newark, and Philadelphia. Although they were less likely to be lynched in the North, the black people who fled the South were sometimes subjected to violent attacks.

In 1919, the United States experienced a series of race riots that collectively approximated a race war.[60] I do not use that language lightly. James Weldon Johnson, an author and civil rights activist, referred to this time as the "Red Summer." He used the term red because of the blood orgies that occurred in more than thirty cities—in each instance, whites beat and killed black people. In some instances, black people fought back, but, outnumbered and outgunned, more blacks than whites lay dead in the nation's streets.

The first riot took place in Charleston, South Carolina. On the evening of May 10, 1919, Isaac Doctor, a black man, allegedly pushed Roscoe Coleman, a white Navy sailor, off a sidewalk. A group of white sailors and civilians chased Doctor. He escaped to a nearby house. A fight took place there, with blacks and whites throwing rocks, bottles, and bricks. A black man fired four gunshots into the air to disperse the crowd. That was a mistake. Rumors quickly spread that a black man had shot a white sailor.[61]

Between one and two thousand white sailors—joined by civilians—stole .22 caliber rifles from a local shooting gallery and "started on a hunt shouting, 'Get the Negroes.'"[62] For several hours, the white rioters took control of the downtown business streets. They beat and shot black people indiscriminately. Trolley poles were pulled down to stop the streetcars and "negroes on the cars were beaten up. One negro was shot down as he was snatched off a car."[63] Black people fought back with their fists and guns. The rioting stopped when Charleston's mayor requested a detachment of U.S. Marines to restore order. In the end, five white men and eighteen black men were seriously injured, and three black men, Isaac Doctor, William Brown, and James Talbot, died of gunshot wounds.

The last of the Red Summer riots occurred in Elaine, Arkansas. It was more a massacre than a riot. On September 30, 1919, approximately one hundred African Americans met in what is today Morningstar Church to form a local chapter of the Progressive Farmers and Household Union of America. They were sharecroppers working on the plantation farms of some of the wealthiest landowners in Phillips County, in the Arkansas Delta. The sharecroppers, who often worked entire years in debt servitude, wanted fair wages. Inside the church, they prayed, sang, and talked; they positioned a couple of armed men in front of the church.

In the early 1900s, black people living in small, rural southern towns were expected to accept their lowly position in society, and they were always expected to show deference to white people. The prospect of black sharecroppers—or any black people—organizing to demand higher pay and better working conditions angered whites. The presence of armed black guards fed into the widely circulating rumor that black people in Elaine (who outnumbered whites nine to one) were planning an "insurrection."

The fear of a black insurrection partially explains the presence of three white men who pulled up to the front of the church. One of the white men looked at the black guards and said, "Going coon hunting, boys?" Gunfire erupted. It is not clear who fired the first shot, but the black guards shot to death W.A. Atkins, a white security officer from the Missouri-Pacific Railroad, and injured Charles Pratt, the county's white deputy sheriff.

The next day, a posse arrived to arrest the suspects. The arrests were made without incident; however, this did not satiate the local whites, who were angry that black people had fought back. A call was sent to whites in Mississippi and Tennessee to come and crush the perceived insurrection. Within a day, more than a thousand armed whites had arrived in Elaine.

They conducted a reign of terror: killing any black person they found. It was an orgy of death. Some black residents fled, while others armed themselves in defense. Five white men were killed, but no one knows how many black people were killed; the estimates range from 100 to 240. As was typical during the Jim Crow period, the only men prosecuted for these events were 122 African Americans, with 73 charged with murder.

The Red Summer riots/massacres were not confined to the South. Beginning July 19, 1919, white civilians and soldiers in Washington, DC, responding to the rumored arrest of a black man for raping a white woman, began four days of mob violence against black individuals and businesses. The local police refused to intervene, so black people defended themselves. When the riots ended, five black people and ten white people had been killed. That was rare. In most twentieth-century race riots—especially during the first half of the century—black deaths exceeded white deaths. In the weeks and months before the Washington, DC, riot, whites attacked blacks in Annapolis and Baltimore, Maryland, and Scranton and Coatesville, Pennsylvania. However, none of these race riots rocked the nation as much as the riot that occurred in Chicago, Illinois.

Although Chicago did not have an ordinance prohibiting blacks and whites from sharing a beach, it was understood that black people would confine themselves to a beach that paralleled 25th Street, and white people would have a beach that paralleled 29th Street. On July 27, 1919, Eugene Williams, a black teenager, crossed the imaginary boundary. Almost as soon as he began swimming on the "white side," white men pelted him with rocks. It is not clear if a rock rendered him unconscious or if he panicked, but he drowned. When police officers arrived, black witnesses pointed to the assailants, but the officers refused to arrest any of the white men; instead, they arrested a black man. Angry crowds gathered on both the "white beach" and the adjoining "black beach." Soon, fighting broke out between blacks and whites. With each incident, the violence escalated. It continued for five days. James Buhrman, a salesman traveling through Chicago, said:

> I was down on the South Side when the worst fighting took place. It was awful. Negroes were being chased and shot down as if they were Huns. I don't know what got into the people. Maybe the hot weather had something to do with it. At any rate it was the worst man hunt I ever saw and I have been over there. What made it seem

so bad was that it was on the streets and in the second largest city in the United States. The end isn't in sight, either. The Chicago Black Belt has sworn vengeance and there will be the dickens to pay when they start to get even. Some of the negroes were as bad as the whites but most of the chasing that I saw was done by the white citizens, who used bricks, clubs and anything they could lay their hands on to kill the negroes.[64]

One widely distributed newspaper story was accompanied by the headline, "Black Invasion of Whites' Beach Causes Trouble."[65] This article, and similar ones, fed the fear that Chicago faced a *black peril*—hordes of ignorant, immoral Negroes overrunning and destroying white communities. The message was clear: whites were justified in using violence to protect white spaces.

In the end, fifteen whites and twenty-three blacks were dead, and more than five hundred people (about 60 percent black) injured. During the riots, white mobs torched the residences of black people, leaving more than one thousand black families homeless. The riot lasted for five days. In its aftermath, some Chicago political authorities proposed—and newspaper editorials endorsed—a system of formal (de jure) segregation in Chicago. Alderman Terence F. Moran introduced a resolution that called for the racial segregation of public accommodations.[66] It did not pass; however, the riot and the later calls for officially sanctioned segregation demonstrated that the North was not so different from the South when it came to attitudes toward black people.

With a century's hindsight, it now seems that the Red Summer of 1919 was almost inevitable. In cities like Chicago, which had an increase in its black population from 44,000 in 1910 to more than 109,000 in 1920, there was inadequate housing for the migrating black people, and the housing that was available was substandard. Equally important, the housing was near recently immigrated Europeans, many also poor. The mutual resentment of the "immigrants" from the South (black people) and the immigrants from Europe was heightened by competition for jobs.

When the United States entered World War I in 1917, thousands of black soldiers enlisted.[67] Although they did not receive fair treatment at home, they trusted President Woodrow Wilson when he said, "out of this conflict you must expect nothing less than the enjoyment of full citizenship rights—the same as are enjoyed by every other citizen."[68] For the men who came from Hampton to Ferris, the war was not an abstraction; it was a reality. Many of them enlisted, including Gideon Smith, Percival Prattis, Percy Fitzgerald, Ernest F. Anderson, Edward P. Bouldin, Virgil L. Haskins, and Dewitt Ellsworth Allen. Like other black men who fought during World War I, they hoped to prove that they were patriotic Americans who deserved to be treated as first-class citizens. But when the war ended, they returned to an angrier version of Jim Crow—all the old indignities plus resentment toward black people in military uniforms. President Wilson had misled them. There was, however, an important change—these men returning from war were more likely to defend themselves against white aggression.

The young men who came from Hampton to Ferris in the early 1900s were aware of the state of race relations. Their lives spanned the Jim Crow era. They did not have the luxury of being unaware. They drank from *colored* water fountains, watched movies in *colored* movie theaters, played on *colored* beaches. They read newspaper editorials claiming that educated black men were likely to engage in criminal behavior. They saw talented, smart black people pretend to be dumb so that they did not offend the Jim Crow demands of white people. They knew butlers and house cleaners, who, in a different nation at a different time, would have practiced medicine or earned livings from behind university lecterns. They knew about lynchings, riots, and massacres. They came to Ferris Institute hoping for the opportunities denied them in many parts of the country. They excelled in their studies. These were smart men. They became, almost to a person, accomplished in their professional fields; moreover, they grew into civil rights leaders, working to end the Jim Crow hierarchy and other expressions of racial injustice.

Tom Shanahan, a sports journalist, claimed that Woodbridge Ferris, inspired by reading Booker T. Washington's *Up from Slavery*, established a "unique working relationship" between Ferris and Hampton.[69] The origins of the agreement—indeed, the agreement itself—have been lost; however, it is clear that from 1910 to the mid-1920s, more than fifty African American men came to Ferris from Hampton.[70] Shanahan claimed that Smith was "one of those otherwise anonymous students."[71] Those students may have been anonymous to Shanahan, but many of them had lives of distinction—and several helped shape the nation's direction.

Shortly after beginning this research, Franklin Hughes said to me, "You're not going to believe the accomplishments of some of the Hampton/

Ferris people." He told me about Percival L. Prattis, who attended Hampton from 1912 to 1915 and graduated in 1917 from Ferris Institute. On February 3, 1947, Prattis, by then a famed newspaper reporter, became the first black news correspondent admitted to the House and Senate press gallery in Washington, DC. His accomplishment occurred two months before Jackie Robinson broke the Major League Baseball color barrier, both events were groundbreaking. The more we researched the life and accomplishments of Prattis, the more we discovered about other Hampton/Ferris students.

Belford Lawson attended Hampton from 1916 to 1919 and Ferris in 1919–1920. He went on to a distinguished legal career highlighted by the distinction of being the first African American to win a case before the United States Supreme Court. Percy A. Fitzgerald attended Hampton in 1917 and graduated from Ferris in 1920. Before his dental career blossomed, he was a supply sergeant for the 369th Infantry Regiment—the Harlem Hellfighters—during World War I. Russell A. Dixon attended Hampton from 1918 to 1920 and finished his undergraduate education at Ferris in 1924. After becoming the first African American to earn an advanced degree in dentistry from Northwestern University, he served as dean of the College of Dentistry at Howard University for thirty-five years. William I. Gibson attended Hampton from 1915 to 1920 and was a student at Ferris in 1922. He had a distinguished career as a newspaper journalist. He also served as the executive editor for Johnson Publishing, the company that published *Ebony*, *Jet*, and *Tan* magazines.

We do not know with certainty why the "arrangement" ended between Hampton and Ferris. The Great Depression likely played a role. It is also plausible that the ascendancy of Hampton as an academic institution meant that African American students in Virginia no longer needed to attend a college preparatory school in the North. Also, Woodbridge Ferris's death in 1928 meant that the institute's greatest champion for racial equality no longer guided its work.

This is a book about those young African American men who left Hampton Institute to study at Ferris Institute between 1910 and the mid-1920s. Our goal was to unearth, contextualize, and share their stories with this generation—people who benefit from their accomplishments. It is also an opportunity to focus on the life and work of our founder, Woodbridge Nathan Ferris, who long before it was normative created opportunities for women, international students, and African Americans. Woodbridge Ferris said, "My plea in Michigan—and it will be my plea to

David Pilgrim and Franklin Hughes researching Percival Prattis

the last breath I draw, and the last word I speak—is education for all children, all men, and all women of Michigan, all the people in all our states all the time."[72] The more we researched his life—meaning, his words and actions—the more we realized that he really did mean "all the people," and he meant it at a time when black people were routinely mistreated in this country.

A final word: I hope that this book will also make apparent the important work begun by Franklin Hughes, my colleague and the coauthor of this book. To use a sports metaphor, he ran the first lap—maybe the first two—before I joined the race. Once I caught up, we ran in tandem. Hughes reminds me of Joel Augustus Rogers, the author, journalist, and historian, who contributed much to our understanding of African Americans in the United States. Like Rogers, Hughes is a dogged researcher—and I followed his lead as we painstakingly searched journals, magazines, newspapers, and online sites, using any and every tool to find clues to forgotten stories—stories no longer lost, stories that should no longer be invisible in the murals we paint.

Woodbridge Nathan Ferris, 1907

In a word, the Ferris Institute is an awakener. It is
not a college, it is a great secondary school, that has
for its mission the feeding of the hungry, regardless
of their age, race, and previous condition.

—Woodbridge N. Ferris

Crimson and Gold (Big Rapids, MI: Ferris Institute, 1909), 13.

Making the World Better: Woodbridge Ferris

Woodbridge Nathan Ferris, the university's founder, was a strong advocate for education for all people, regardless of race, ethnicity, or sex. This commitment was evident in his words—and in his actions. While serving as president of Ferris Institute, he was confronted by a landlord who complained that she had been insulted. The source of her insult was that she believed Woodbridge had "sent to her boardinghouse a colored girl."[1] The landlord informed the founder that the other roomers—all white females—were prepared to leave the boardinghouse unless the student was removed. Woodbridge reluctantly found the student another house. He then challenged the entire student body:

> On the following morning I said to the School that I supposed I was living in Michigan, but I concluded, after describing this experience, that I was living in Louisiana. The Ferris Institute is one of the most democratic schools in the United States. It has no color line; it has no age limit; it has no educational requirements for admission. It is open to every man and woman, every boy and girl who are hungering for an education. This makes the attitude of the girls of this particular boarding house all the more remarkable.[2]

He shared this story publicly, which he likely found difficult. Ferris Institute was, after all, his life's work. He could not force the landlord to rent a room to the student, but he could help the student—and he could send the message to the Ferris student body that racism was wrong, that it was inconsistent with his vision of the institution. This incident occurred in the early 1900s, a time when most American whites supported—openly or tacitly—a racial hierarchy *and* the beliefs that buttressed it. Woodbridge's actions were based on his belief that respecting the dignity of others is a foundation of a moral society.

Ferris Institute was nearly destroyed on February 21, 1950. A fire devastated the campus, burning down the two chief buildings: Old Main and Old Pharmacy. The institute's rise from the ashes is evidence of the resiliency of the campus community—and testimony to the foundation laid by Woodbridge and Helen Gillespie Ferris, his wife, the institute's first teacher. The fire and its place in the university's history are well-documented, but there was a lesser known fire that is also significant. On November 22, 1926, a Michigan newspaper reported:

> Nine students of Ferris Institute narrowly escaped death Monday
> when flames swept a dormitory occupied by Negroes. The building
> that burned was turned over to the Institute several years ago by
> Senator Woodbridge N. Ferris for use of the Negro students.[3]

Woodbridge knew that black students, including the ones who came from Hampton, often had difficulty finding rooms to rent. So he bought a building and had it converted into a small dormitory. It is likely that he used personal funds to purchase the building and then donated it to Ferris Institute. We do not know much about the fire—its origins or aftermath—but we can reasonably infer that the creation of the dormitory was another example of Woodbridge endeavoring to create an institute where Jim Crow era black people could get the education they needed to rise in this country. Why was Woodbridge so out of step with the prevailing racial attitudes and behaviors of his time? Although there is no clear and definitive answer, there are clues to the origins of his racial egalitarianism and commitment to social justice. And the first clue is to be found in his upbringing.

Woodbridge was born on January 6, 1853, to John Ferris Jr. and Estella (Reed) Ferris, on a farm near Spencer, New York, in Tioga County. He was the first born, and after him came five girls and another boy.[4] His parents were of "exemplary morals and character" but "extremely poor in worldly goods."[5] The family spent the first ten years of Woodbridge's life in a one-room log cabin built by John. They only bought from stores what they could not produce from the land or make with their hands. Early on, poverty shaped their lives—without embittering them. Later Woodbridge said:

My father and mother directed the most important part of our education. I learned obedience, diligence, thrift, sobriety, honesty; in
fact, all the virtues that ever adorn a noble manhood.[6]

Woodbridge's mother was literate; his father was not. John referred
to himself as "an ignorant uneducated man."[7] That assessment was too
harsh. He could not read, but he valued knowledge. John made sure the
children attended the district school. Woodbridge read newspapers to him.
When prominent orators spoke in or near Spencer, John went to hear their
ideas—and he took his son, cultivating in Woodbridge a lifelong interest
in understanding the human condition and a desire to relieve human
misery. His parents modeled the commitment to serving others. Estella
cared for sick and ailing neighbors and gave the "less fortunate" what they
needed. Woodbridge said of his father:

> Possessing the fundamental virtues of greatness, he awakened in
> his children abiding regard for the priceless virtues of a noble char-
> acter. His condemnation of wrongdoing was of the sledge hammer
> type. His neighbors recognized his leadership, his sterling integ-
> rity and his enthusiastic willingness to help any human being who
> would try to help himself.[8]

The students who came from Hampton to Ferris were talented and
hardworking, but they were black at a time when most white Americans
were certain that black people were inherently inferior. They left their
communities in the Jim Crow South, becoming quasi-refugees in their
own country. In a society that exalted whiteness, their black skin made
them, in a real sense, less fortunate. Woodbridge was drawn to them, to
their plight, their talents, and their willingness to help themselves. When
he helped them and others to rise, he was continuing the legacy of his
parents: help those who are trying to help themselves.

It is likely that Ferris was also influenced by the abolitionists he heard.
His early schooling was in Spencer, Candor, and Oswego, all towns in
New York reputed to have been stations on the Underground Railroad. In
1871, he enrolled in the Oswego Normal and Training School. Before the
Civil War, Oswego was a hotbed of abolition activity. Local advocates gave
fiery antislavery speeches, wrote letters to newspapers attacking slavery,
formed abolitionist societies, signed petitions to be sent to Congress, and,
most significantly, hid runaway slaves and helped them create new lives

This picture of Frederick Douglass hangs in the Multicultural Student Services Office at Ferris State University.

in the North or travel to Canada. Gerrit Smith, a wealthy landowner, sheltered fugitive slaves and gave forty-acre plots of land to black people. Silas W. Brewster used his general goods store and home as stations on the Underground Railroad.[9] John C. Harrington's home had basement tunnels for hiding runaways. John B. Edwards and Lydia Edwards hid blacks fleeing enslavement. In 1860, John wrote, "A smart colored man, Henry, arrived here last evening. I will see to getting him underway for Canada."[10] There were others—many others—in Oswego County who used their words and their actions to oppose the enslavement of black people.

While in Oswego, Ferris attended many lectures, including at least one given by Frederick Douglass, one of the most influential antislavery voices.[11] Unlike the white men and women who spoke against the enslavement of black people, Douglass had been enslaved, had legally been another man's property. After several failed attempts, he escaped to New York City in 1838. As a runaway, he was guilty of refusing to be a slave. William Lloyd Garrison, a prominent abolitionist, said of Douglass:

> He stood there as a slave—a runaway from the southern house of bondage—not safe, for one hour, even on the soil of Massachusetts— with his back all horribly scarred by the lash—with the bitter remembrances of a life of slavery crowding upon his soul.[12]

Garrison wrote those words in 1842, as Douglass was beginning his ascent as a national figure. In the years that followed, the man whose back was scarred became a powerful and persuasive speaker—so gifted that some whites refused to believe that he had been enslaved. His eloquence as a speaker and writer undermined the narrative that enslavement was necessary, because black people did not have the intelligence to live as free citizens. Thousands of white Americans read Douglass's autobiography, *Narrative of the Life of Frederick Douglass, an American Slave*.[13]

As a "free" man living in the North, Douglass was often rebuffed when trying to enter "white spaces"—eating-houses, steamers, even religious revival meetings. He bitterly complained that his entrance was blocked with these words, "We don't allow niggers in here."[14] Douglass had been opposed to the gradual abolition of slavery—and after Emancipation, he demanded that immediate steps be taken to grant black people the rights held by free people. The formerly enslaved, he argued, should be treated as first-class citizens, free from insult, segregation, exploitation, and terrorism. Slavery was a crime against humanity, and so was Jim Crow. This was Douglass's message in 1871, the year that an eighteen-year-old Ferris sat in an Oswego audience and listened to the brilliant man who was born enslaved.[15] A quarter of a century later, students at Ferris Industrial (not yet Ferris Institute) listened to Principal Ferris praise Douglass's life and work.[16]

By the beginning of the twentieth century, Ferris's admiration of Douglass was without controversy; however, his praise of John Brown was—in a word—radical. Brown, a white abolitionist, was willing to kill to stop the enslavement of black people. He saw himself as an instrument of

God charged with leading a holy war, an insurrection, to end this affront to God and humanity. Brown believed that slavery was an evil system supported by immoral men—men who deserved to die. In 1858, Brown and his sons led small-scale attacks that resulted in the deaths of several people who supported bringing slavery to Kansas. This battle reinforced Brown's conviction that slavery could only be ended by armed conflict.

Brown set about building an army of insurrectionists. He envisioned arming slaves across the South so they could wage war against their enslavers. In 1859, Brown and twenty-one of his followers attacked and occupied the federal armory, arsenal, and rifle factory in Harpers Ferry, Virginia (now West Virginia). Their goal was to get weapons. The plan was thwarted by local farmers, militiamen, and marines led by Colonel Robert E. Lee and Lieutenant J.E.B. Stuart. Most of Brown's men were killed or captured. He was hanged. The raid was a turning point in the nation's history, away from compromise and toward war.

John Brown was, for many years, one of the most vilified figures in United States history. He was dismissed as a madman, a religious fanatic who justified murdering innocent white people. It says a lot about Woodbridge Ferris's views on slavery—and racial justice—that he praised the militant abolitionist. In 1902, while delivering a speech at a banquet in St. Louis, Ferris applauded Brown's courage:

> John Brown belonged to the advanced guard of heroes in the Civil War. John Brown possessed the courage that conquers. He hated slavery and he had the courage to express his hatred in a way that awakened the conscience of the American republic. Lincoln possessed the same courage mellowed by the divine charity of the Master.[17]

Douglass was not the only black man to influence Ferris's thinking about race, race relations, and racism. In 1903, W.E.B. Du Bois published *The Souls of Black Folk*, a classic work of American literature and a cornerstone of African American protest.[18] In this collection of essays, he persuasively argues that it is beneath the dignity of human beings to beg for rights—including the right to an education—that should belong to all people. Black people, he said, should not follow the lead of Booker T. Washington, whose emphasis on material progress and acceptance of segregation amounted to the submission of black people to the domination of whites. Du Bois's ideas were considered radical and incongruent with the everyday functioning of the United States. But the ideas were not too radical for Ferris; he read excerpts from *The Souls of Black Folk* to the Ferris Institute student body the year it was published. Washington and Du Bois struggled to find common ground, but Woodbridge made his peace with both:

> I commend most heartily the magnificent work of Booker T. Washington. He is training men and women to become useful and indispensable in the great industrial world. Du Bois adds to Booker T. Washington's program a higher claim. If I understand him, he would never fail, even in a country school to give the boys and girls an appreciation of the poetry, music and painting of the masters. Take out of life its poetry, its painting, its drama, and there is little left worthwhile.[19]

Booker T. Washington

On July 16, 1902, a man identified as "William Ody, a negro" was burned at the stake in Clayton, Mississippi.[20] He was accused of attacking Virie Tucker, daughter of a prominent planter. According to newspaper accounts, the white woman was out riding in the country when she was "so violently pulled from the buggy by the negro that both of her lower limbs were broken."[21] Although at least one account claimed that she was raped,[22] most reports concluded that Ody, alarmed by the woman's screams and the presence of a white physician who happened upon the scene, fled "before his purpose was accomplished."[23] News spread rapidly. *A Negro brute had attacked a white woman.* A posse pursued him. Citizens rushed to Clayton from nearby towns. Ody was captured and brought before the woman, who positively identified him. Ody asserted his innocence. His captors promised him a safe escort to a nearby jail and a "regular trial," but "they were met on the outskirts of the town by an armed mob, which took charge of the prisoner."[24]

The mob meant to punish him, to make an example of him.[25] Cans of oil were procured, and piles of rich pine wood gathered. Ody was taken to a spot near the scene of the alleged assault. A bonfire was built adjacent to a tree. He was told to prepare for death. Realizing that he was to be burned to death, Ody "begged piteously for mercy."[26] It was late, nearly midnight, when James Tucker, Virie's father, set the fire.

> The blaze threw a lurid light over the faces of the 500 men who stood watching the ghastly spectacle. Ody made no outcry. The

contortions of his body alone showed the terrible agony he was suffering. In fifteen minutes it was over. The shooting at the charred remains and the scramble for souvenirs of the awful affair which have marked so many crimes of this kind in the South were omitted. When the flames subsided the burned body was left hanging by the chain which held it to the tree and the mob dispersed quietly.[27]

The next day, almost eight hundred miles north of Ody's lynching, a different audience of white people also traveled, with great excitement, to lay hands on a black man. However, they did not come to harm him; no, they came to Big Rapids, Michigan, to shake his hand, to listen to a man widely celebrated for his approach to dealing with race relations. The Big Rapids *Pioneer* reported:

> An audience of over eight hundred gave Booker T. Washington, of Tuskegee, Alabama, a hearty greeting as he stepped upon the platform of the Ferris Institute auditorium last evening to deliver his address on "The Negro Problem." Mr. Washington has wrought a great work for his race, and the desire to see and hear a man who has worked up from slavery to the presidency of an educational institution of world-wide renown for its earnest, common sense methods of schooling a people who have to begin with the question of earning a livelihood, was manifest in the application for tickets from Cadillac, Howard City, Fremont, Mecosta, Reed City, Evart, and other surrounding towns. None were disappointed.[28]

On the day he lectured at Ferris Institute, Booker T. Washington was the most famous and most influential black man in the United States, widely celebrated as a great educator. He was the face and voice of many African Americans. His lofty status was remarkable given his humble— even degrading—start in this world.

Washington was born enslaved on a small tobacco plantation in Franklin County, Virginia, between 1856 and 1858. On the plantation inventory he was listed, along with cattle, tools, and furniture. He was valued at four hundred dollars. His life, in his words, "had its beginnings in the midst of the most miserable, desolate, and discouraging surroundings."[29] His mother Jane worked as a cook for James Burroughs, their enslaver. Washington never knew his father, though he heard rumors that his father was a white man from a nearby plantation. Fortunately

Booker T. Washington and his traveling party were photographed during a 1906 trip through the Southwest. Chester Bush (third from right) and John Bush (fourth from right) joined Washington (sixth from right).

for the young boy, he was born near the end of the American system of enslavement.

After emancipation, Washington's family traveled to Malden, West Virginia, where Jane joined her new husband, Washington Ferguson, who had escaped slavery and fled to the Mountain State during the Civil War. Like most of the newly freed black people, the family was poor. Washington went to work in the salt furnaces and coal mines with his stepfather. Eventually, he succeeded in convincing his stepfather to let him attend a few hours of school. At school, he claimed for himself the family name Washington (up to that time he was known only as Booker).[30]

Washington worked in salt furnaces and coal mines for several years. At the age of sixteen, he made his way east to Hampton Institute where he worked as a janitor to pay for his studies. He was an exemplary student, mentored by Samuel C. Armstrong, the institute's president. After completing his education at Hampton Institute, he taught and flirted with the study of law and the ministry. A teaching position at Hampton decided his future. In 1881, Armstrong recommended Washington to become the first leader of Tuskegee Institute, the new normal school (teachers' college) in Alabama.

Washington's lecture at Ferris Institute, like many of the talks that he delivered, focused on his work as leader of what is today Tuskegee University. He was a twenty-five-year-old teacher at Hampton Institute in Virginia when he received the invitation to come to Tuskegee, a city in Macon County, Alabama, to open a school for black teachers. When he arrived, he discovered that the Alabama Legislature had appropriated two thousand dollars to pay teachers to work at the school—but no other funds were provided. There were no teachers and no buildings to hold classes. Undeterred, Washington opened the school on July 4, 1881, in a "rather dilapidated shanty near the coloured Methodist church. . . . Both the church and the shanty were in about as bad condition as possible."[31] A year later, the school was moved to the grounds of a vacant plantation that Washington had purchased. After his lecture at Ferris, the *Pioneer* wrote:

> Starting in 1881, with one teacher and thirty students, and in a rented building, the institution had in attendance last year 1384 students, representing 30 states and territories, Cuba, Porto Rico and Jamaica. All except a small number sleep and board on the grounds. Ninety officers and teachers are employed. Graduates and undergraduates to the number of 4,000 are doing most valuable work all over the South as industrial leaders, teachers, etc.[32]

Tuskegee Institute was Washington's answer to the "Negro Problem"— the question of what should be done with millions of impoverished black people and how to handle the relationship between blacks and whites in the South. The institute was the embodiment of Washington's philosophy of self-help and accommodation. In the early years of the institute, teachers and students made bricks and used those bricks to construct classrooms, barns, and outbuildings. The students needed food, so they raised livestock and grew crops. This work provided for the students' basic needs, while simultaneously teaching them job skills. Generations of Tuskegee students were taught trades, while also being taught hard work, thrift, enterprise, and delayed gratification. Washington believed that this approach would win the support and respect of whites and lead to black people being fully accepted as people and citizens. Du Bois was not impressed.

As Washington began to attain stature as leader of his new, small, and struggling school at Tuskegee he gave total emphasis to economic progress through industrial and vocational education. He believed that if the Negro could be taught skills and find jobs, and if others could become small landowners, a yeoman class would develop that would, in time, be recognized as worthy of what already was their civil rights, and that they would then be fully accepted as citizens. So he appealed to moderation, and he publicly postponed attainment of political rights and accepted the system of segregation.[33]

Washington walked a difficult path. There were many whites, especially in the South, who did not want *any* education for black people. They believed that education spoiled black people—made them unfit for and rebellious against the jobs open to them. Why, they asked, should a white man's taxes pay for the education of a black man or woman who, once educated, would no longer want to plow in a cotton or tobacco field, cook a white man's meal, wash a white woman's clothes, clean a white family's house, or say "Yes, sir" to a white man? Senator Ben Tillman of South Carolina traveled the nation telling audiences that "somebody has to pound it into their [black people's] heads that they were put on earth to pick cotton."[34] His colleague, Coleman Livingston Blease, a South Carolina senator, boasted that he was unalterably opposed to spending even a penny on educating "baboons and free niggers."[35] Tillman and Blease were two of many influential white southerners who believed that education for black people—even vocational training—was a threat to the racial hierarchy.

Washington also had to deal with increasingly angry people in the black community, including the Talented Tenth—voices that demanded that black people push not only for Washington's economic equality but also argue and fight for the right to vote, the dismantling of racial segregation in housing, education, public accommodations, and the military, and the end of mob lynching.

Washington went to great lengths to convince southern whites that he was not advocating social equality. His most famous speech—the one that thrust him into the national debate on race—was delivered on September 18, 1895, to a predominantly white audience at the Cotton States and International Exposition in Atlanta. It is often referred to as the Atlanta Compromise Speech. In his speech, Washington promised whites that if they helped black people, they would be rewarded with loyal, nonthreatening servants who would not resist Jim Crow segregation.

> Casting down your bucket among my people, helping and encouraging them as you are doing on these grounds, and to education of head, hand, and heart, you will find that they will buy your surplus land, make blossom the waste places in your fields, and run your factories. While doing this, you can be sure in the future, as in the past, that you and your families will be surrounded by the most patient, faithful, law-abiding, and unresentful people that the world has seen. As we have proved our loyalty to you in the past, in nursing your children, watching by the sick-bed of your mothers and fathers, and often following them with tear-dimmed eyes to their graves, so in the future, in our humble way, we shall stand by you with a devotion that no foreigner can approach, ready to lay down our lives, if need be, in defense of yours, interlacing our industrial, commercial, civil, and religious life with yours in a way that shall make the interests of both races one. In all things that are purely social we can be as separate as the fingers, yet one as the hand in all things essential to mutual progress.[36]

The year before he came to Big Rapids, Washington was embroiled in a national scandal. On October 16, 1901, President Theodore Roosevelt extended a last-minute invitation to Washington to join him for dinner. The next day, the White House released a statement announcing that the dinner had occurred. The response from southern politicians and the southern press was immediate and nasty. The *Memphis Scimitar* stated, "The most damnable outrage which has ever been perpetrated by any citizen of the United States was committed yesterday by the President when he invited a nigger to dine with him in the White House."[37] The newspaper added that Washington is "a nigger whose only claim to distinction is that, by comparison with the balance of his race, he has been considered somewhat superior."[38] Senator Tillman went further, claiming, "It will require the killing of 1,000 niggers to reduce that race to its proper place after Booker Washington's dinner in the White House."[39]

The southerners were fearful of what they derisively called *social equality*, meaning that black people would have the same status as whites with no barriers to the participation of black Americans politically, educationally, economically, or socially. This was the white southerners' worst nightmare, an end to the Jim Crow racial hierarchy. They screamed in fear that this dismantling of de jure and de facto discrimination would result in "Negro domination" and interracial sex. One southern newspaper wrote:

> By this act President Roosevelt has affronted every decent white man in America. He has given the stamp of his approval to social equality, and proclaimed to the world that the son of Booker Washington is good enough to be the son-in-law of Theodore Roosevelt. And in this opinion I concur with Mr. Roosevelt. The truth is, I have more respect for the blackest, rankest-smelling chicken thief in Mississippi than I have for the occupant of the White House. . . . I have contended all along that social equality was the end to which Washington and his pusillanimous ilk were striving. He has advised the members of his race to so live, accumulate property, educate themselves, and when they should become fortified and entrenched that they could then enforce the recognition of their rights. . . . It is a declaration of war. The gauntlet has been thrown down before the South, and the South will not be slow to take it up. For nearer and dearer to every Southern white man than life is the assurance of his superiority to the race that has been the slave of slaves from the beginning of history and which served him and his father in the most menial capacities. . . . [T]he white man who does not hold himself the racial and social superior of the negro is lower than negro.[40]

The bitter, angry attacks, with accompanying racist language, lingered. Six months after the dinner, a poem, "Niggers in the White House" appeared in newspapers across the nation. It continued to be published through 1903.[41] Woodbridge was aware of the controversy—aware of the foul, thick hatred directed toward Washington (and Roosevelt); nevertheless, he invited Washington to Ferris Institute. Why? Because he admired Washington, believing him to be "a great man."[42] He read Washington's *The Story of My Life and Work* to the Ferris Institute student body on multiple occasions.[43] Woodbridge believed that the students' education was enhanced by listening to the words of the nationally known educator who had been born enslaved.

In 1902, when Washington came to Ferris Institute, Woodbridge's views on race relations were still evolving. He had long opposed the Jim Crow era mistreatment of black people, but he was still trying to determine the best approach for addressing the nation's race problem. He was sympathetic to Du Bois's harsh critique of the way that black people were treated in the United States. But Du Bois's talk about a Talented Tenth—stressing the need for educating the ablest 10 percent of black people—must have been offensive to Ferris, who believed that higher education should be accessible to all people. Like Washington, Ferris had built an institution that focused on practical education—learning that produced men and women who were ready to work. Ferris respected Du Bois's intellect, but he admired Washington as a builder committed to the common man and woman. Washington died on November 14, 1915. There were memorial services nationwide, including in Detroit. Most of the eulogizers qualified their praise of Washington by referring to him as a great Negro, or a great Negro educator, but Ferris—who offered the eulogy at the Detroit memorial—referred to Washington as "the prince of American educators."[44]

Phrenology

For much of his life, Woodbridge Ferris embraced tenets of phrenology, a pseudoscientific theory of human personality introduced in 1796 by Franz Joseph Gall, a Viennese anatomist and physician.[45] Gall and his followers claimed that one's brain was made up of distinct organs responsible for different emotional and intellectual faculties—attributes and abilities. Use of a particular organ in the brain impacted its size. If one, for example, regularly used the brain organ that controlled temperament, that organ grew—less used faculties shrank. The skull was malleable, its shape and contour changed to accommodate changes in the brain's surface—providing an indirect reflection of the brain, and, thus, the dominant features of one's character.[46] The shape of one's head revealed one's intelligence and character. Phrenology was one of the earlier disciplines to correctly recognize that different parts of the brain have different functions. However, the belief that bumps and depressions in the cranium are reflective of personality and skills was incorrect.

Ferris spent much of his life searching for an understanding of human behavior, in part, because he wanted to create a template for human improvement. If the phrenologists were right—the brain was like a muscle that could be exercised—then a good education would grow the brain and strengthen intellectual faculties. This meant that all people, regardless of their backgrounds, could improve their character and intelligence. This appealed to Ferris. He understood that phrenology was not a science, but he hoped that it contained insights beneficial for living a productive life.

Phrenology was popular in the 1800s, so it is not surprising that people searching for a scientific basis for white supremacy found it useful. François-Joseph-Victor Broussais, one of Gall's disciples, declared that Caucasians were the "most beautiful," and that Australian Aboriginals would never become civilized, because they lacked a cerebral organ for producing great artists.[47] Proslavery supporters argued that areas located toward the top and back of a human's skull were large in Africans—therefore, they were easily tamed and enslaved.[48] Phrenology, though debunked as a science, maintained some popularity into the Jim Crow period, particularly among white segregationists. Fortunately, Ferris's search for understanding about the human condition was not limited to, or even primarily driven by, his attraction to phrenology.

A key influence on his thinking was Franz Boas, the leading anthropologist of the twentieth century and a fierce opponent of ideologies of scientific racism. Boas maintained that differences in human behavior are not primarily determined by innate biological dispositions but are the result of cultural differences acquired through social learning. He argued against racial hierarchies *and* the beliefs about race that undergirded them. Race, for Boas, was primarily a social construct. His theory of cultural relativism discredited prevailing beliefs that Western civilization was superior to simpler societies. Ferris said:

> Prof. Boaz [*sic*] has convinced me that inborn racial differences are few and worthy of little consideration. Any attempt to show that there is a natural gulf between the colored race and the white race must result in failure. No one questions the existence of an artificial gulf between the two races—a man-made gulf. This man-made gulf has mitigated against the progress of both races in America. This gulf has established class distinctions. In a democracy class distinctions are odious, are perilous. Our ten million colored people are with us. They are not here because they sought this country as a haven for rest, but because they were brought here in bondage to the white race. The Civil War banished chattel slavery, but it is too early in American history to declare that a subtle slavery has not been substituted.[49]

43

Woodbridge Ferris on the campaign trail (c. 1912).

Public Speaking

Woodbridge Ferris was a gifted orator who spoke before hundreds of audiences. His style was the "heart to heart talk," with a recounting of his personal experiences and a "philosophy expounded which had grown out of these experiences."[50] His folksy style was well-received at high schools, colleges, professional conferences, teacher symposia, churches, campaign rallies, and political rallies. One observer said of him, "He is a true orator. He speaks with a purpose, and with most telling effect."[51] Near the end of his life, a local newspaper assessed him as an orator:

> Senator Ferris says he is not famous, is not a great orator, is not a pessimist, but he is famed among Chautauqua and lyceum folk for giving lectures which are entirely within the grasp of the average listener and yet so filled with genuine food for thought that they are never forgotten. Ferris's humor is accidental, not intentional; his irony and sarcasm are inherited; his practical sense is the result of his educational, religious, and political knockdowns. In education, religion and politics he is a radical. Those who are searching for a man with a real message will find in Senator Ferris a man who instructs, awakens and inspires.[52]

Typically, he began with praise for his audience, entertained them with self-deprecating humor, and then offered old-school insight on contemporary issues. In many of his addresses, he talked about the nobility of work. For him, education was not to be seen as a way to avoid work. One should embrace work not escape it. Work, especially work with one's hands, was necessary for personal growth—was even a way to honor God. Hard work, manual work, ennobled people and made them better. He said:

> There is no quicker way to lose a paradise if you have one, than to try to live without work; and there is no surer way of gaining one than by work. And I mean by work, manual work—at least some manual work. I have said, a thousand times or more, that bank officials, schoolmasters, doctors, lawyers, and preachers, would be better men by doing manual labor—some manual labor, daily. Show me a man with flabby muscles, and I will show you a man with a flabby Will— and Will is the motor power of life. But not for this alone should they do manual labor. The touch with the tool, with the sod, is a touch with the millions who toil, by whose sweat the earth produces—a humanizing touch with the great brotherhood of humanity.[53]

Ferris's speeches dealt with an eclectic collection of topics, among them, success, arithmetic, teaching, marriage, parenting, practical education, and great men and women. Abraham Lincoln was one of his heroes; indeed, Lincoln was likely the person that he admired most. He saw in Lincoln a man who has faced almost impossible circumstances, yet found the courage to make difficult choices—decisions that resulted in saving the nation at the cost of hundreds of thousands of lives. In 1922, at a club banquet in Ann Arbor, Ferris was presented with a painting of Lincoln.[54] The gesture moved him. He believed that Lincoln was, to put it succinctly, great, and he shared his affection for Lincoln with audiences.

> Without a moment's hesitation I say Abraham Lincoln is entitled to be called the greatest American. The Declaration of Independence is the greatest exposition of the American ideal. Abraham Lincoln was the incarnation of that idea.[55]

Ferris's most popular speech was titled "Making the World Better."[56] That simple phrase served as the official (later unofficial) mission of the university that he founded. Although the particulars of the talk varied depending on the setting, the main themes remained consistent: avoid selfishness, do not oppress others, and help all who are willing to help themselves. Here is an excerpt from that speech as delivered in 1910:

In order to make the world better we must first make ourselves better. We must curb selfishness, and the best way to do that is to start on ourselves right in our own homes. Selfishness gets its first hold on us in our homes; consequently that is the place to begin uprooting it. The man who is very selfish and who at the same time has a sharp intellect is a very dangerous man. It is not the ignorant man who is to be feared, but the sharp, selfish one, who has no righteous principles. Get all the knowledge you can, but use your knowledge in the right way and it will be of untold benefit to you. Don't use it in oppressing others. . . . And when you see a man or woman trying to rise and doing the right thing don't be selfish but try to help that person rise.[57]

Ferris as Politician

Woodbridge Ferris had a stellar political career. In 1904, he was an unsuccessful candidate for Governor of Michigan against Republican Fred M. Warner. Although he lost the election, the campaign increased his name recognition and popularity across the state.[58] In 1912, he became the second Democrat to be elected governor of Michigan since the formation of the Republican Party in 1854. His election was the result of both infighting among Republicans and his popularity—the Republicans won all other statewide seats, Progressives finished second in those races, and Democrats finished far behind.[59] Nicknamed the Good Gray Governor, he served consecutive two-year terms, from 1913 to 1917. One observer summarized Ferris's time as governor this way:

> Teachers have become governors of states, but doubtless the greatest example of this kind of great school teacher is the highly regarded ex-governor of the big state of Michigan, Woodbridge N. Ferris. No governor was ever more beloved. No governor of any state more keenly realized the duties of his high office or set a higher example in moral methods than the chief executive of that state.[60]

As governor, Ferris—who once described himself as "constitutionally a radical, a natural born fighter, prone to favor extreme measures"—supported reforms in the state. He pushed for the popular election of senators, a corrupt practices act, more power for the state government over public utilities, and the creation of institutions for treating people with tuberculosis and epilepsy.[61] Easily the most controversial decision of his term was to send the state National Guard to settle a violent copper mine strike in the Upper Peninsula. In a letter to William Sulzer, another governor who found himself under siege, Ferris said, "Any governor who calls out the militia to protect life and property must take his medicine. He at once divides the populace."[62]

Governor Woodridge Ferris, 1915

Ferris used the governor's office to advance civil rights for black people. In the early decades of the twentieth century, a dominant societal narrative was that black people were not significant contributors to the country. In 1914, Governor Ferris was informed that black community leaders in Chicago planned to stage an elaborate event highlighting African American history and achievement in the fifty years following the end of enslavement. The event—the National Half Century Anniversary Exposition and the Lincoln Jubilee—was to be held in Chicago, from August 22 to September 16, 1915. The event would feature exhibits from several states.

In July 1914, Ferris designated a commission populated by black people to serve as delegates to the exposition. The commission, headed by Charles Warren, was tasked to "organize an exhibit showing inventions, handiwork, science, and art of African American life in Michigan."[63] The body was also charged with creating "a manual showing the professional, political, and religious achievements of citizens of this state in whole or in part of Negro descent."[64] The book they produced is called *The Michigan Manual of Freedmen's Progress*.[65] It includes a statistical portrait of blacks living in Michigan, biographies of prominent blacks, photographs of black-owned homes, businesses, and farms, and a catalog of contributions to the Jubilee exhibit. The manual remains a source of pride for black people living in the state. More than seventy years later, the *Detroit Free Press* offered this assessment:

MICHIGAN EXHIBIT, INVENTOR McCOY AND HIS DEVICES, LUBRICATING OIL CUPS.

GENERAL VIEW OF MICHIGAN EXHIBITS.

The Michigan exhibits at the 1915 Lincoln Jubilee are pictured. Elijah McCoy is shown in the top booth photograph. The bottom photograph features a painting of Woodbridge Ferris with an "Our Governor" caption, painted by William Ross Roberts.

The book is a testament to blacks' accomplishments, filled with stories of men and women who had made their mark, whose lives were woven into the fabric of the state. Featured were people in every line of work: lawyers, farmers, chemists, merchants, doctors, actors, detectives, policemen, nurses, singers, inventors, barbers, contractors—and a man who sold souvenirs to tourists at Sault Ste. Marie.[66]

Michigan's participation in the Lincoln Jubilee was a huge success. The Michigan display was the best of the exhibitions—and the same can be said of the manual produced by the Michigan contingent. Governor Ferris attended the event on "Michigan Day," delivering a speech supporting the event.[67]

The National Half Century Anniversary Exposition and the Lincoln Jubilee occurred the same year that white Americans were packing theaters to watch D.W. Griffith's epic *Birth of a Nation*.[68] Based on Thomas Dixon Jr.'s novel *The Clansman*,[69] the film starts from the premise that freeing blacks from enslavement was a horrible mistake. Without the constraints of slavery, the innate savagery of blacks, especially black men, was directed against virginal white women. In the minds of Griffith and Dixon, the South, maybe the entire nation, was headed for Negro domination—until the Ku Klux Klan rode in and saved America for white people.

The black people in *Birth of a Nation* were caricatures: loyal mammies and toms, childlike sambos, and most prominently, raping brutes. These fictional representations were in blunt contrast to the hardworking, overachieving, and family- and community-minded black people at the Lincoln Jubilee. Ferris found *Birth of a Nation* a movie without any redeeming value.

> It is the most damnable thing I ever witnessed and not for $50.00 would I sit again for three hours and watch such scenes. If it were in my power to do so, I would issue an order today not to allow this picture to ever again be shown in the state of Michigan. The *Birth of a Nation* is not only an insult to the colored race, but it is an insult to the intelligence of the white race as well.[70]

Ferris's condemnation of *Birth of a Nation* was consistent with his conviction that he must oppose white supremacy and the racial prejudice that undergirded it. Although he still believed that there were differences between the races, he did not believe that those differences were significant in any meaningful way. In a speech given at a peace conference at Mackinac Island on July 21, 1914, he addressed racial hatred:

> Thank God! in my own veins there is not a drop (allowing me to be the judge) of race hatred. I know of no man of different color or of a different race whom, retaining his manhood, I am not willing to sit beside at the table or to work with wherever and whenever the work demands the co-operation of two men. Thank God! I have been born destitute of anything that savors of race hatred! I would not emphasize the matter of the belligerent instincts in man were it not for the fact that in almost every state of the Union there has grown up the feeling that the white race has the divine right to earth. Thank God, I haven't that feeling; and so far as I have any influence or power, I hope to teach men that God Almighty must have had wise object in creating different races, with innate differences and yet intending us all to partake of the richest bounties of the earth and live together in peace and joy for the righteous ends of life.[71]

In 1922, Ferris was elected to the United States Senate. He rarely made speeches in the Senate, but he was an indefatigable worker in committees—education, foreign relations, library, and post offices. Most notably, he supported the establishment of a federal Department of Education.[72] In 1924, while serving as a delegate to the Democratic National Convention, his name was placed in nomination for the presidency by A.M. Cummins of Lansing.[73] He described Ferris as "a man whose honest high purpose and courage have been proven beyond all question," and then added:

> Forty years ago there came to Michigan a poor man in purse, rich only in enthusiasm of his desire to be helpful to mankind. This man was always and in all things a fundamental Democrat, always a believer in the desire and purpose of the people to do the right, if not mad dupes of demagogues on the one hand or special interests on the other. He was always a crusader for righteousness in public and private life.[74]

Those words of praise were echoed the following year in a newspaper article published in advance of Ferris delivering a speech at the Fifth Street Methodist Church in Harrisburg, Pennsylvania. The writer summarized Ferris's life and work:

Senator Ferris is an educator, a great statesman and an orator. For many years he has been an educator and head of the Ferris Institute. During these years he has impressed upon his students the value of clean living, clear thinking, civic righteousness and real service. His administration as governor of Michigan was characterized by these same high principles. His election to the United States Senate is due to his dominating personality and his years of unquestioned loyalty and integrity in the affairs of that great state. His life has been an open book, he is an idealist, a vigorous champion of the right, and always a foe to fraud and sham.[75]

Last Year

On January 28, 1928, Woodbridge and Mary McLoud, his second wife, left Washington for Hampton, Virginia. William H. Scoville, the grandson of Henry Ward Beecher, the abolitionist whose sermons helped shaped Ferris, met them at the train station. The Ferrises were escorted to the home of Hampton's principal, James Edgar Gregg, and his family. In the evening, they joined almost two thousand people in Ogden Hall to listen to the singing of spirituals—and short speeches by Francis G. Peabody, James E. Gregg, Robert R. Moton, and James Scattergood—all Hampton trustees. On Sunday morning, the Ferrises and the Gregg family attended church. It was Founder's Day. That evening, Ferris spoke at Ogden Hall. He remembered:

> I spoke for forty-five minutes on the subject, "Give American Youth a Chance." In my lifetime I have addressed many audiences, but no audience more enthusiastic and appreciative than this one.[76]

After his talk, the Ferrises were given a tour of Hampton. Woodbridge had wondered how much mechanical ability existed among the students. He found exceptional students doing excellent work in all departments. Although he had helped educate several dozen Hampton students at Ferris, it is likely that this was his first trip to the institute. And he was impressed:

> After visiting the Hampton Normal and Agricultural Institute, I was able to understand how Booker T. Washington had become inspired as a student at this institution and how Tuskegee Institute, under his magic hand has developed into a wonderful institution

for the education of the Negro. . . . I say without hesitation that the Hampton Normal and Agricultural Institute is one of the greatest schools I have ever visited.[77]

Woodbridge was born a free man at a time when others were enslaved. He spent his early adulthood trying to discern human nature—and then the rest of his life using his words and actions to combat white racism. In the end, his answer for the race problem foreshadowed the words of Martin Luther King Jr. a half-century later.

The colored people have been extraordinarily patient and forbearing. The question of questions is how can they best secure the rights and privileges that belong to them? Any influence that savors of hate is ruinous. The one regenerating power in the world is love. Love is not a racial factor. It is a universal factor, that makes for patriotism, that makes for democracy. This is the only influence that can save the world from race hatred, that can save a nation from disintegration.[78]

"Senator Ferris 'Very Sick Man.'" "Senator Ferris Critically Ill." "Senator Ferris Is Near Death." Those were the headlines across the country on March 17, 1928. Ferris, who had not been active on the Senate floor for a couple of months, was suffering from bronchial pneumonia. His condition was pronounced "very grave" for a week. Oxygen was administered artificially.[79] Members of his family were summoned to the Washington hotel where he made his home in the capitol. A team of doctors offered little hope that Ferris, then seventy-five years old, would recover. They were right.

On March 23, 1928, two months after visiting Hampton, he died. It was exactly eleven years after his first wife had died. All businesses and schools, including Ferris Institute, were closed in Big Rapids the day of the funeral. Many of Michigan's elected officials, including Governor Fred W. Green, attended the funeral. Six military companies and the 126th Infantry Regiment Band marched in the funeral cortege to Highland View Cemetery in Big Rapids, where Woodbridge and Helen Ferris are both interred. Reverend Alfred W. Wishart preached the eulogy. He said of Woodbridge:

He was a bold, aggressive champion of high ideals. His influence was that of all true men who uphold real values and contend for righteousness and justice. A multitude of men and women scattered over this country are with us in thought today. To them Senator Ferris was the guide and example of their youth. In time of moral or material need he was their friendly counselor and benefactor. When life was hard for them he helped them solve their problems. To invest one's influence in the lives of struggling youth is glorious living, and gloriously did our friend live.[80]

After he died, Ferris's place in the Senate was taken by Arthur Vandenberg, editor of the *Grand Rapids Herald*. Vandenberg established a reputation as a voice of opposition against President Roosevelt's New Deal programs. He was a leading conservative from the Depression through the Soviet-American conflicts. Vandenberg did not have Ferris's commitment to civil rights. The *Baltimore Afro American* compared the two senators:

> The consensus, however, is that Vandenberg has not been as generous toward colored folk as was his predecessor, the late Senator W.N. Ferris, whose unexpired term he was appointed to fill. Senator Ferris is best remembered for his affiliation with the Ferris Institute, which was most liberal to colored students.[81]

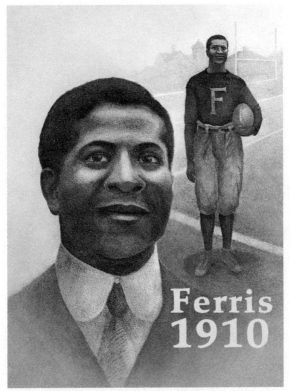

Gideon E. Smith painted by Diane Cleland, 2017.

The colored player has had to show that he could take it—that he had intestinal fortitude of the highest order.

—Bill Gibson

"Hear Me Talkin' To Ya!" *Baltimore Afro American*, November 16, 1935, 21.

Ready to Play: Gideon Smith

Gideon Smith wanted to play big-time college football. There is something exhilarating about scooping up a ball and sprinting ninety-five yards toward the end zone—your legs made lighter by a roaring crowd . . . or pushing by a giant lineman to sack a quarterback . . . or outfighting several opponents to cradle a game-saving fumble. Smith had these experiences and many others, but his career as a player for Michigan Agricultural College (MAC)—today known as Michigan State University—almost never began.

> When Smith decided to go out for football in 1912, MAC Coach John Macklin wouldn't issue him a practice uniform, effectively preventing Smith from joining the all-white Aggies—or so Macklin thought. But after a future teammate's friend—a veterinary student named Chuck Duffy—loaned Smith his old high school uniform, Smith reported for practice and eventually won Macklin over with his rugged play.[1]

Smith may have won Macklin over, but he was not allowed on the varsity team until the following year; he spent that first season playing with the MAC freshman team. When Smith joined the varsity team in 1913, he became the institution's first black varsity athlete in any sport—and helped pave the way for African Americans to play intercollegiate football on previously all-white teams at other universities. Smith starred on the MAC team from 1913 to 1915.

He first received nationwide acclaim after MAC defeated Michigan 12–7, on October 11, 1913. That was the MAC team's first victory over their in-state rival. Hailed as one of the country's best collegiate left tackles, Smith occasionally starred as a running back.[2] In a 1915 football game against Marquette, he "moved to the backfield long enough to score three TDs."[3] After that final season, Smith was named to All-Star teams picked by the *Chicago Daily News* and *Collier's Magazine*. During his three-year varsity career, the team compiled a 17–3 record, outscored opponents 636–123, and twice defeated Michigan. He was selected to the Michigan State Athletics Hall of Fame in 1992.

His play on the football field gained him a measure of acclaim experienced by very few African American athletes during the Jim Crow period. After graduating from MAC, he became a successful college coach at Hampton Institute, where he led the football team from 1921 to 1940. During those twenty years, his teams compiled a record of 97–46–12, including a Colored College National Championship in 1922. Smith's exploits as a star football player and a successful coach are well-documented; however, not enough attention is given to the role that Ferris Institute played in his life.

Gideon Edward Smith, sometimes referred to as George Smith,[4] was born on July 13, 1889, in Norfolk County, Virginia. His parents were John and Patience L. Smith.[5] Little is known of John, other than that he was born in Virginia. It is likely that he died young, leaving Patience a widow. She was born in 1850. In the 1900 Census, she and three of her children—Margaret, fifteen; Mary, thirteen; and Gideon, ten—were all listed as "servants" in a household headed by W.L. Wilson, an unmarried white farmer.[6] Another child, John Elliott, was away from home, attending Hampton Institute.

The Wilson home was in Pleasant Grove Township, in Norfolk. All of the children attended Norfolk public schools.[7] At some time before 1910, the Smiths moved into a small house that abutted the Wilson home. Patience and her children remained servants—field hands on the Wilson farm—however, her youngest child Gideon had replaced John Elliott at Hampton Institute. And "replaced" is the right word. The family could not afford to have two children at Hampton at the same time; therefore, Gideon had to wait until his older brother was graduated before he could continue his education. In a letter to an unnamed benefactor, Gideon wrote:

> Two years before coming here I used to hear about people up North paying the student's scholarship, and I used to wonder if anybody would ever pay mine. Then the next thing was getting here for

someone to pay my scholarship. I used to get a letter of encouragement from [my] brother every month telling me to study hard so I
could enter the school when he finished. I studied as he had told me,
but that constant study had seemed to get dull, and it didn't look
as if he would ever finish. After seven years he finished the Postgraduate course in Agriculture. The next fall after he had finished
he brought me to school.[8]

In 1905, when Gideon was sixteen years old, he enrolled in Hampton
Normal and Agricultural Institute. Like his brother, Gideon was a work
student in the boarding school, meaning that each day he did farmwork to
pay for his tuition and room and board. In the benefactor letter referenced
above, Gideon said:

Last year I worked in the cow barn. My work was milking. There
were ten of us in the barn, and we had twelve cows apiece to clean
and milk. This was a very easy job, for we used to get through our
work, and at the house by nine o'clock in the morning. Then we
would go out again at one o'clock, and work until five, or sometimes
till six in the afternoon. At half-past seven we would go to school,
and stay there until 9 o'clock.[9]

Hampton's approach was to teach the students through manual
labor—and to use the labor of the students to help sustain the school.
In the early 1900s, many of the students at Hampton received instruction in trades: blacksmithing, carpentry, clocksmithing, farming, harness
making, printing, tailoring, painting, and wheelwrighting. This was called
a practical education, in part, because it steered black people to become
gainfully employed and self-supporting as industrial workers, artisans, or
farmers—and it guided them away from careers that were direct threats
to Jim Crow segregation.

Smith studied at Hampton Institute for five years; then, desiring a
higher education than Hampton offered, he enrolled at Ferris Institute.[10]
In 1910, Ferris was, in the words of one its students, "neither college nor
high school" but "a school that has all the best features of both."[11] Like
Hampton, Ferris offered practical, career-based educational paths, but
the paths were different. Hampton steered its students toward studies
that resulted in jobs open to black people; Ferris offered other educational
paths—for example, civil service, commercial preparation, and college

The 1911 Ferris football team. Gideon Smith (second row, far right) and Top Taggart (top row, second from right) were the team's star players.

preparatory—majors that led to "white jobs." Smith enrolled in Ferris Institute's college preparatory program.

He came to Ferris looking for academic opportunity and found it; he was graduated in 1912. He discovered something else: football. It did not take long for anyone watching to realize that Smith was a good athlete with a passion—even a joy—for the game. Before enrolling at Ferris, he had not played organized football. Of course, one could argue that the Ferris Institute football team was not well organized. According to the 1910 yearbook:

> After a rather unsatisfactory season, in the fall of 1907, the formation of a regular Ferris Institute football team was abandoned, and for the season of 1908 no regular Ferris Institute team existed, although each of the larger departments, the Commercial, College Preparatory and Pharmacy departments organized department teams and played a series of exciting and strenuous games. . . . Shortly after the last game the Mount Pleasant team, which had made a wonderful record for the season, asked for a game with the Institute. Although, up to that time no single team had been organized Mr. Pickel picked a

Gideon Smith (top row, far left) was a member of the 1911 Ferris Institute band.

team from the three departments and with a week's practice held the strong Mount Pleasant team to a score of 11 to 0; a much better showing than many of the State college teams had made. A second game was arranged with Hope College. As the Hope College coach, a Carlisle Indian, played against us, we have no need to apology for our showing.[12]

Shoulder pads and headgear were in short supply. Players had to supply their own uniforms. No two players wore jerseys that were the same color. One of the players said, "We were a pretty ragtag looking outfit, but this gave us no complex. . . . The boys loved the game."[13] It was likely that Smith learned from several of the more seasoned players, especially W.C. "Top" Taggart, who was a player and de facto coach during Smith's tenure—and later became Ferris's first paid football coach.[14]

Even as a novice, Smith excelled on the playing field. In one of his first games, Ferris trailed 3-0 at halftime against a Grand Haven, Michigan, independent team but came back to win 11-3. Smith was singled out by the local newspaper: "Every man played a brilliant game especially Smith on the Line."[15] The next season, Ferris played Alma College, at that time a strong team. Ferris lost 15-5 in a bruising game viewed by the largest crowd that had watched Ferris play. A newspaper reported, "Smith, the colored star player of the F.I. Team received a bad jolt in the jaw, which necessitated taking out time. . . . The invulnerable Smith again lost his wind but was up and playing directly."[16]

In the last game of the 1911 season, Ferris Institute played the MAC freshman team. The game was played in inclement weather, and the clay field was covered with water. The play was sloppy, with lots of punts and fumbles. MAC won the game 11–0. This game introduced Smith to big time (or soon to be big time) college football. The next year, he was a player on the MAC freshman team. It is not clear if Smith played on the 1912 Ferris Institute football team. He may have played one or two games before moving on to MAC.

Smith learned to play football at Ferris Institute, but he did not gain fame as a gridiron star until he joined the MAC Aggies. In 1912, while playing on the Aggies freshman team, Smith "played a fine defensive game" and scored two touchdowns in a scrimmage against the Aggies varsity team.[17] His performance alerted observers to his skill and likely impact once he was allowed to play with the varsity. According to the *Lansing State Journal*, the work of the "colored tackle" was "phenomenal," adding "his presence on the line is expected to be a world of benefit to the Plow Boys."[18]

The next year, in a game against the Olivet Crimson, Smith recovered a blocked kick in the end zone for a touchdown. It was the team's first points of the season. With Smith excelling on defense—and carrying the ball on offense—MAC won 26–0.[19] A local newspaper praised Smith's performance:

> Smith's work was perhaps the most noticeable. It was his first varsity game, and the big colored fellow covered himself with glory. He made the first touchdown, never failed to gain when he carried the ball, and was a tower of strength on defense.[20]

In the next game, the Aggies routed Alma 57–0. Again, Smith scored the first touchdown. This was the first time that Smith had been on the winning side against Alma; his Ferris teams lost to Alma in 1910, 55–0, and in 1911, 15–5.[21]

The following week, MAC defeated the University of Michigan team in a grueling game that at times devolved into organized violence. Blake Miller, one of the stars on the MAC team, was carried off with a dislocated vertebra, the result of a late and dirty hit. The Aggies scored two touchdowns—after each score they failed to convert the extra point—and held on to win 12–7. The win left the student body euphoric. A thousand "joyously raving students" rushed the field and "quickly grasped the team and lifted them to shoulders. Like the conquering heroes they were, the Aggie team was borne in triumph."[22] The *Lansing State Journal* praised the Aggie linesmen, "Beginning with Herman Schultz at left end and going through the whole list of lineman you have names of stars. Schultz, Smith and Leonardson on the left stopped Michigan attack repeatedly."[23]

On October 25, 1913, the MAC team defeated Wisconsin 12–7.[24] In some ways, this win was more impressive than the defeat of Michigan. In 1912, Wisconsin reigned as champions of the Western Conference, with a record of 7–0, and their 1913 team had many of the same players. Smith was outstanding against Wisconsin. According to the *Lansing State Journal*:

> Smith the colored boy, who played left tackle, was a star of the first magnitude. Playing against Butler, the All-American tackle of last year, Smith made his heavy opponent look like a dirty deuce in a new deck. He stopped the mighty rushes of Cummings, Tormey, and Van Ghent and his tackling was sure and low. He broke up many of Juneau's best plays and on one occasion intercepted one of Bellow's forward passes and raced down the field 20 yards before being downed. Modest and unassuming, Smith accepted the praises that were showered after the game. "I worked as hard as I could to help the other boys win. I'm glad for the sake of the team, Coach Macklin and M.A.C that we won." Smith's great playing was the talk of Madison fans Saturday night as it was predicted before the game that Butler would wear him out before the contest was finished.[25]

The MAC Aggies finished the season 7–0, outscoring their opponents 180–28. Chicago and Harvard claimed to be national champions, but the Aggies would have been competitive against either team. Aggie fans had to be satisfied with the knowledge that their team was undefeated; they had defeated a strong Wisconsin team and Michigan, a longtime powerhouse and their intrastate rival. The MAC players were heroes in the Lansing area and throughout the state. Smith, selected to the All-Western Second Team, received high praise from many quarters. Walter Eckersall, one of the first great college players, said of Smith, "He will develop into the most famous tackle that ever played on a Western gridiron."[26] Woodbridge Ferris, then governor of Michigan, attended the game against Michigan.

He wrote a letter to Smith, published in many newspapers, which included these words:

> I want to congratulate you upon the splendid work you have been doing in the football team. Your friends at Ferris Institute read of your success with delight. I like you for two reasons. First because you are a man and you have a wholesome ambition for doing your work well. Second, I like you because you are a success at football. Go ahead. I am sure that you are now realizing in a measure your ambition, and I am also sure that the future is rich with promise for you. I might go further and say that I congratulate M.A.C. upon having a man of your ability in their team, a man who reflects credit upon himself and upon his fellow associates.[27]

Woodbridge Ferris's assessment of Smith was not shared by some—maybe most—of the players who faced Smith on the playing field. Foreshadowing the abuse that Jackie Robinson would face a generation later, Smith endured "a barrage of verbal abuse from opponents."[28] Like Robinson, Smith endured racial harassment without retaliating.[29] Blake Miller said that the racial epithets hurled at Smith across the line of scrimmage by opponents were unrepeatable.[30] Fans also shouted racist slurs at him. One newspaper article details the challenges faced by Smith—they erroneously refer to him as "George Brown."

> Brown is the first colored boy who has worked out at East Lansing in some time. There are many difficulties in his way, and because of his color there is a bit of prejudice against him. This is not openly shown at the school, but has been in all the games in which he has played in the surrounding towns. He never pays any attention to remarks made to him, and has won the favor of his teammates by his gentlemanly conduct.[31]

The mistreatment of Smith extended beyond the playing field. When the Aggies played road games, hotel clerks tried to prevent him from staying with his teammates. When the Aggies played the Wisconsin team in Madison, Coach Macklin and the white players registered to stay in a hotel, then sneaked Smith into the hotel through a fire escape. Smith remained in the room until game time, "comrades bringing his meals to him from a nearby restaurant."[32] At other times, Coach Macklin gave him money for food and lodging in a nearby black community. Smith would

In this picture of the 1915 MAC varsity team, Gideon Smith (top row, third from left) stands next to Coach Macklin. Picture used with permission of Michigan State University Archives and Historical Collections.

later join his teammates at practice, in the game, and on the train ride back to Lansing, Michigan. These whites-only hotels were evidence that de facto segregation existed in the North.

Reporters often evoked and tapped into racial stereotyping when they wrote stories about Smith. They rarely spoke of him without mentioning his race or skin color. He was described as "the Ethiopian," "the negro tackle," "the dusky player," "the chocolate-hued member of the Michigan Aggies," even, "the elongated negro tackle."[33] Although he was roughly six feet tall and never weighed more than 180 pounds, many accounts describe him as "the big Negro tackle." That description was not harmless. In the early 1900s, there were thousands of newspaper depictions of so-called Black Brutes—large, dark-skinned black criminals.[34] Although Smith "played big," he was not particularly large—and his aggression was confined to the football field. One historian noted, "Even by the standards of the early pros, Gideon Smith was not a large tackle."[35]

In many stories, Smith is quoted using so-called Negro dialect, even though his use of spoken English was indistinguishable from what one heard from his teammates, opponents, or reporters. As he neared his final game in 1915, Smith was quoted in a newspaper article—one that purported to celebrate "the big fellow"—saying, "No mo' football fo' me."[36] A few months later, another newspaper discussed whether Smith would leave Michigan to go to Tuskegee Institute in Alabama to become a coach. In the article, Smith is made to sound like a minstrel show performer.

> "Ah'm considering the mattah very carefully," the big boy remarked to his friends today, "but ah just haven't made up ma mind. It looks like a good thing, but I suah do hate to leave old Michigan. She's been mighty good to me."[37]

Another story—one which received national attention—centered on Smith's apparent disdain for playing with a helmet. In the early 1900s, helmets were not mandatory for college football players and not all players wore them, but this story seems to validate the stereotype that the heads of black people were harder than the heads of white people.

"Negro didn't need any head guard"

Lansing, Mich., Oct. 18—Michigan Agricultural college students have among them a football man who scorns head protectors. He is G.E. Smith, colored tackle on the Aggie team. "Here, Smith, don't you want a headgear?" asked Coach Macklin of the dusky player just before a scrimmage yesterday. "A helmet for me? No, sir," replied Smith with a smile. "My head is harder than any helmet." Smith is the only negro player on any of the Michigan college elevens.[38]

Revealingly, some newspapers altered Smith's language. In the account carried by the *Daily Missoulian*, the last section of the "Head Guard" story is rewritten with Smith using Negro dialect: "'A helmet for me? No, sah,' replied Smith with a grin. 'Mah haid's harder than any helmet.'"[39]

The "hardheaded Negro" joined the "chicken loving buffoon" as two of many anti-black portrayals found in jokes, lectures, speeches, sermons, and newspaper stories in the early 1900s. Despite his success on the football field, Smith did not escape these racist depictions. After the triumphant 1913 season, members of a local African American church feted Smith with song and food, including "fricasseed chicken and pastry dainties."[40] Some newspaper reports tainted this celebratory event.

"Dusky tackle up in ranks of race; football his sport"

Gideon F. Smith negro, who as left tackle for the Michigan Aggies, helped the team to victory on the gridiron during the past season, was gorged with fried chicken by the members of the African Methodist church of Lansing the other day. Smith played against Mount Union when the east end college team journeyed to Michigan.

"Mistah" Smith's colored brethren were devoted football fans during the season and occupied front seats in the bleachers wherever he was scheduled to play. Their lusty cheering and quaint coaching was one of the hits of the season. The negro minister in a laudatory speech at the banquet table referred to Smith as "among Michigan's most prominent representatives of the colored race."[41]

The success of the 1913 team brought the MAC Aggies and Smith national attention. The 1914 season was not as successful for the team; however, Smith remained a dominant player. The Aggies lost to Michigan 3–0 in a punishing defensive struggle. A newspaper reported, "Smith, the colored tackle, was a snag in Michigan's course on more than one occasion. The big Negro is very fast and he seemed to be at the bottom of the pile every time the Wolverines tried a line play." Another writer added, "While Smith, the colored tackle, played a brilliant game on the line, he failed to make worth-while gains when called upon to carry the ball."[42] This was an anomaly. Although Smith was more valuable to the Aggies as a defensive player, he was a proficient, sometimes starring, ball carrier during an era when tackles were allowed to run the ball. Smith had no problem carrying the ball against Akron on October 31, 1914. He recovered a fumble and ran ninety yards before being stopped just short of the goal line. Later, he scored on a sixty-yard run. MAC won the game, 75–6.

The Aggies finished the season 5–2. Not only did they lose to their intrastate rival, Michigan, but they were also defeated by Nebraska 24–0. Moreover, they struggled in a 21–14 win over tiny Mount Union—a victory helped by a crucial interception by Smith. He received his second varsity letter. In 1913, he had made the All-Western Second Team—one could argue that he should have been on the First Team—but he was left off all All-Star teams in 1914.

Smith played his final season of varsity football in 1915. The team only played six games and finished with a 5–1 record. They crushed Alma 77–12, and Smith was a star on the line. They defeated Carroll 56–0. Smith scored two touchdowns. Despite the lopsided margin of victory, the team did not play a good game. Smith's play was "the one redeeming feature."[43]

All was forgiven the next week when the Aggies defeated Michigan 24–0. Although he was injured during the game, Smith was the dominant player throughout the contest. The score was not indicative of the dominance displayed by the Aggies. The *Detroit Free Press* called it "a massacre, a rout, an annihilation."[44] After applauding Smith's running ability—he "gained frequently and fluently"—they described his impact on defense:

> When it came to the defense, Smith, the big M.A.C. tackle, was far and away the best man in the game. This large person is a decided brunette, as to complexion, but as a football player he is pure gold all the way through. The way he ripped that Michigan offense—or what would have been the Michigan offense if she had had any—to pieces was a caution. No matter where the Maize and Blue sent its plays, there always seemed to be a dark man in the way. According to the score-card, there was just one Smith in the game but to the spectators it seemed that there must have been about 20 of the destructive breed right in the path of Michigan's best plays. Not only did Smith pulverize the Wolverines on defense but he carried the ball himself from position now and then and got away with a couple of good runs.[45]

The high of beating Michigan was not sustained; in the next game, the MAC Aggies were dominated by Oregon State, losing 20–0. Oregon State used unusual line formations and shifts to confuse the Aggies. They also double- and triple-teamed Smith, which may explain how he suffered an injury—cracked ribs. Smith bounced back in his final game, against Marquette, when he scored three touchdowns. That game capped a distinguished career. His coach Macklin—and Jessie Harper of Notre Dame and Fielding Yost of Michigan—voted him All-American. He was selected to the 1915 All-Western team and First Team in the *Sullivan in the News* voting. MAC graduated him in 1916.

Smith played one football game after finishing the 1915 football season. It was a single contest—but the game (and Smith's role in it) is etched in the annals of American professional football. In the first three decades of the 1900s, the Canton Bulldogs were a dominant team. They played in the Ohio League from 1903 to 1906 and 1911 to 1919, and the American Professional Football Association—renamed the National Football League in 1922—from 1920 to 1923 and again in 1925 and 1926. In 1915, the Bulldogs, led by Jim Thorpe, were scheduled to play the Massillon Tigers, whose star players included Knute Rockne and Charlie Dorais. The game would decide the Ohio League Championship. Jack Cusack, the Bulldogs coach, wanted an "insurance policy" so he signed Gideon Smith—under the alias Charlie Smith. Although Cusack signed Smith—probably on the recommendation of George "Carp" Julien, one of Smith's MAC teammates who was on the Canton team—it is clear that Cusack was ambivalent about playing a black player. Gideon later reflected on that day:

> The coach looked at me kind of funny when he came into the dressing room. He didn't start me. That was all right, because I never had seen much football from the stands and I was enjoying it. But he sent me in to start the second half, and I stayed. After the game Jim Thorpe, who was on my team, came over and said, "Boy, I wish you were in there all the time. They don't pay quite so much attention to me when you're in the game." I guess that was about the nicest compliment I ever had, coming from an athlete like Jim Thorpe.[46]

At the beginning of the second half, Canton led 6–0, on the strength of two field goals by Thorpe. In the game's most critical play, Smith recovered a fumble in the end zone to secure the victory. Because he played in the game, Smith has the distinction of being the last African American to play professional football prior to the formation of the National Football League—in 1946, Marion Motley, Bill Willis, Kenny Washington, and Woody Strode signed professional contracts.[47]

Smith began life after football by serving a brief stint in the military. He returned to Virginia and became a teacher at the West Virginia Collegiate Institute—today named West Virginia State University. He later served as a teacher at the Virginia Normal and Industrial Institute. In 1921, he became the head coach of the football team at Hampton Institute. He held that position from 1921 to 1940 and was the winningest coach in the first ninety years of the institute. His teams won five CIAA football championships and ten track and field championships. In the last years of his professional life, he became the athletic director at Hampton.[48]

Carl McClellan Hill was one of the many Hampton football players coached by Smith. Hill, who later served as president of Hampton, said of Smith, "He was a man of such integrity. I learned so much football and character from him."[49] Those words could have been offered by any of the hundreds of young men coached by Smith. By all accounts, he was a modest, soft-spoken man who cared deeply about improving the lives

Gideon Smith (third row, far left) coached the 1921 Hampton Institute football team.

of young people. After his playing career ended at MAC, he could have remained in Michigan; however, he returned to the segregated South to mentor a generation of young African Americans.

In 1961, Ferris State College awarded Smith a distinguished alumni award. The honor was bestowed because of his success as a football player and coach. It was not his only award. In 2014, Smith was named the American Football Coaches Association's recipient of the Trailblazer Award, an accolade created to honor early leaders in the football profession who coached at historically black colleges.

As with the other young African Americans who came from Hampton to Ferris to further their education, Gideon Smith was born and lived during the Jim Crow period—a time when black people were treated as inferior to white people intellectually, culturally, athletically, and in all ways that mattered. Although they did not escape all racial prejudice by coming to Michigan, they did receive opportunities denied to them in Virginia. In 1913, Smith was featured in an advertisement for Ferris called "What School?" It is a testimony to Smith's impact on Ferris Institute—and

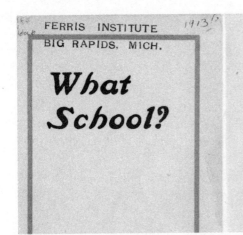

FERRIS INSTITUTE 1913

BIG RAPIDS, MICH.

What School?

Rogers Rock on Lake George, N. Y.,
July 5, 1913.

I spent twelve months in the College Preparatory Department of the Ferris Institute, and during that time my total expense was $200, most of which I earned while attending the school. Before entering the Ferris Institute I graduated from the Hampton Industrial Institute, Hampton, Virginia.

The Ferris Institute lives up to all that it advertises in its catalog and other publications, and gives every student a fair chance regardless of race or color. Every man is judged by what he does. The morning exercises alone are worth the tuition asked. In these the president and his assistants bring the whole student body face to face with the necessary knowledge of every-day life. The student who listens attentively leaves the Ferris Institute with a broader view of life.   GIDEON E. SMITH.

Gideon Smith is featured in this 1913 "What School?" advertisement for Ferris Institute.

Woodbridge Ferris's commitment to education for all people—that a black man was used in this advertisement. The advertisement represents a testimony of his time at Ferris.

Belford V. Lawson painted by Diane Cleland, 2017.

The Fraternity's record in the struggle for civil rights
shows that in the best multi-talented Renaissance
tradition we have been participants, not silent spectators.
In point of fact, leaders of Alpha Phi Alpha, long have
summoned the people toward the horizon of hope.

—Belford Lawson

"Alpha Phi Alpha and the Civil Rights Revolution," *Sphinx*, Fall 1963, 6.

A Relentless Foe:
Belford Lawson

There is a photograph of the 1920 Ferris Institute class. It shows several hundred students standing in front of the main building. Unlike many photographs taken in the early twentieth century, some of those pictured are smiling or waving, and a few are playfully hugging. The men are dressed in either their Sunday best—a dark suit or suit jacket, white shirt, and tie—or in military uniforms, including doughboy hats, though World War I ended in 1918. It is likely that the picture was taken in the later weeks of the fall, because many of the students wore overcoats.

The photograph is framed, but it does not hang on any wall at Ferris; instead, it lies in a corner, propped against a wall, in the university's archives. That is unfortunate. The picture tells a noteworthy story about Ferris. There are many female students, as many as a quarter of the students pictured. Most were in women-dominated fields: shorthand, typewriting, and kindergarten instruction; however, there were female students in business, commercial, pharmacy, and college preparation. More surprising, there were twenty to twenty-five African American students, some in suits, and others in military uniforms. They were not segregated. They sat or stood shoulder to shoulder with their white classmates. A serious-looking black man sat near the front, between two white students. His name was Belford Vance Lawson Jr., and almost two decades after the Ferris Institute class picture was taken, he became the first African American to win a case before the United States Supreme Court.[1]

Lawson was the lead attorney in *New Negro Alliance v. Sanitary Grocery Co.* (1938), a landmark Supreme Court case that safeguarded the right to picket. He argued at least eight cases before the High Court. Of all the students who came from Hampton Institute to and through Ferris Institute—indeed, of all students who ever attended Ferris—Lawson was one of the most accomplished. His work as a civil rights activist spanned half a century. It is not hyperbole to say that Lawson played a pioneering instrumental role in ending legal segregation in the United States.

He was born on July 9, 1901, the ninth of eleven children. His father, Belford Lawson Sr., was a railroad switchman and his mother, Sarah Hickman, a schoolteacher. The family lived a working-class life in Roanoke, Virginia, until the father left for two decades, leaving the family near poverty.[2] Lawson enrolled at Hampton in 1916, most of his time there was spent in the carpentry program. "While atop a Hampton building hammering nails, he concluded that he was not intellectually challenged. He threw the hammer to the ground and descended a ladder. He aspired for more than manual labor."[3] He remained at Hampton until the spring of 1919; later that year he enrolled in the college preparatory program at Ferris Institute.[4] This was the heyday of Hampton students at Ferris Institute. Among the students were Russell A. Dixon, Maceo Alston Santa Cruz, Virgil Haskins, Charles Jackson, Charles Fisher, Maceo Clarke, and Percy Fitzgerald.

During Lawson's year at Ferris Institute, he was a member of the institute's Reserve Officers' Training Corps (ROTC). He also distinguished himself as an athlete. He and Maceo Clarke, another African American from Hampton, played on Ferris's baseball team.[5] Lawson had his greatest athletic success as a football player, albeit on a struggling Ferris team. In one game against Hope College—a game won by Hope 71–7—Lawson, playing halfback, "made the only successful run for Ferris during the first quarter which netted her eleven yards."[6] He also played well on defense. The Hope student newspaper reported:

> Big Rapids had to leave our town with only one touchdown in her belt, but she showed herself a game loser. Lawson, the colored halfback, altho crippled, played a strong game and drew the admiration of the crowd by his pluck.[7]

It was common for the Hampton students to send letters to their alma mater. These letters, often sent to Hampton's registrar, were, in effect, progress reports. A letter sent by Lawson in September 1919 reveals that he had made an important decision: to become an attorney—one committed to making the world better.

Belford Lawson (second row, second from left) was a member of the 1923
University of Michigan football team. Image used with permission from Bentley
Historical Library, University of Michigan.

There are twelve Hampton boys here and I am glad to say we are
doing splendidly so far. . . . I have decided to take law, as I feel that
I will be of more service in the world in that capacity. All of the
boys wish to be remembered to you. We all feel very grateful to dear
old Hampton in many ways and, personally, I hope someday I can
render some service to Hampton.[8]

In 1920, Lawson enrolled in the University of Michigan. He was a
successful student, earning his bachelor's degree from the College of
Literature, Science, and Arts in 1924; however, his years at the university
were noteworthy for his activities outside the classroom. He was a member
of the varsity debate team. A polished public speaker, Lawson won oratorical awards, including the Atkinson Memorial Oratorical Medal, in "competition with some of the leading speakers and debaters on the Michigan
campus."[9] His fame as a speaker also brought him attention from the local
Ku Klux Klan, who sent a letter telling him he was "too active," should
"stay in his place," and to "speak when spoken to."[10] When asked about
the threat, the young Lawson said, "It doesn't frighten me any."[11]

Years later, a colleague described Lawson as "a superb and gifted
elocutionist, whose profound oratorical skills transformed the spoken
word into a melodic symphony of prose."[12] One writer said of Lawson,
"His oratorical powers have been likened to those of the immortal Daniel

Webster."[13] This was lofty praise. Lawson spent almost a half-century traveling the nation speaking against racial injustice.

Lawson is often hailed as the second African American to play football at Michigan, with George Jewett (1890) being the first. There is a photograph in the Bentley Historical Library at the University of Michigan. It shows the 1923 football team, the national champions. The picture first appeared in the *Michigan Daily* newspaper. Unlike the formal studio photograph of the team, the one in the library includes a black player, Lawson. Why was he not in the official photograph?

It was not because of his performances in scrimmages. In 1922, *Michigan Daily* reporters attended a scrimmage between the Michigan varsity team and the Reserves. Lawson was on the Reserves squad. In the newspaper, he was described as "the big Negro fullback." He was one of several players "who showed up best against the first string athletes."[14] After another scrimmage, the same newspaper stated, "Lawson, the husky negro half back . . . played such a stellar role during his brief stay in yesterday's scrimmage."[15] In a scrimmage against the freshmen team, "Lawson grabbed all of the passes for the Reserves and made long gains every time, one of them for 30 yards."[16] In 1923, the newspaper again applauded Lawson's performance during a scrimmage: "Lawson carried the ball for gains time and again, starting to run the ends and then cutting in, successfully eluding many would-be-tacklers."[17]

Lawson won varsity letters for the football team in his sophomore, junior, and senior years. They were Reserves letters. It is clear that he was a talented football player, especially as a running back. But despite excelling in scrimmages—including contests against the Michigan varsity—he was never allowed to play in an official game.

The coach of the team was Fielding Harris Yost. During his twenty-five seasons as head coach at Michigan, Yost's teams won ten Big Ten Conference titles and six national championships, with a record of 165–29–10.[18] He was an innovative coach who built Michigan into a national powerhouse. But there was a side of Yost that was not admirable. The son of a Confederate soldier, Yost was in the words of one writer, "an egomaniac, a racist and a rule breaker."[19] That is a common assessment among writers who study the history of Michigan football. In *A Legacy of Champions*, the authors wrote, "But one of Yost's blind spots had no redeeming qualities: he was a racist."[20] No black football player played even one down while Yost was the coach—and that included Lawson.

Belford Lawson is seated next to W.E.B. Du Bois (in the light suit) at a 1932 Alpha Phi Alpha banquet. Image used permission of Scurlock Studio Records, Archives Center, National Museum of American History, Smithsonian Institution.

Although triumph on the football field eluded Lawson at Michigan, he did find success with a fraternal order. He became a member of Alpha Phi Alpha, the first African American, intercollegiate Greek-lettered fraternity. The fraternity was founded in 1906 by seven students at Cornell University to combat the isolation they experienced at the mostly white Ivy League school.[21] In 1909, the Epsilon chapter of Alphas was established at Michigan. Lawson joined that chapter in 1922. The next year he was a delegate to the Alpha's general convention in Columbus, Ohio. In the 1930s, at the general convention, he gave presentations criticizing the nation's Jim Crow practices. By 1937, he was general counsel of the organization. From 1946 to 1951, Lawson served as general president of the fraternity, by then recognized as the most prestigious organization for college-educated African Americans. It was also an organization deeply involved in the fledgling civil rights movement. Thurgood Marshall, Charles Hamilton Houston, Paul Robeson, Charles H. Wesley, Walter White, and W.E.B. Du Bois (an honorary member) were Alphas.[22] The organization's commitment to racial equality was evident in a speech that Lawson delivered at the 1946 national convention. His challenge to his fraternal brothers included these words:

> The great decision of this generation of Alpha men is whether we shall, with every ounce of energy, with every dollar in our treasury, with every fiber in our mind and soul, deny the gigantic conspiracy to preserve our segregated status quo, and destroy the mighty,

monstrous mockery of human decency and dignity, the yoke of Jim Crow which hangs around our necks. To compromise is to evade the crucial issue. I call to action! Let us speak for the dawn.[23]

Many of the students who came from Hampton to Ferris joined the Alpha Phi Alpha fraternity. While in college—especially for those attending predominantly white institutions—the fraternity created and sustained a space of safety and belonging; after graduating, it allowed them to be a part of an organization that was committed to the uplift of black people. Gideon Smith was a member for more than three decades. William I. Gibson served on the editorial board of *Sphinx* magazine, the official publication of the Alphas—and the second oldest African American publication in existence.[24] Russell A. Dixon was an Alpha. There were many Alphas, but few were as revered as Lawson—affectionately referred to as "Mr. Alpha."[25]

The fraternity sponsors an annual Belford V. Lawson Oratorical Contest, to honor its namesake and to encourage young orators. The award is dedicated to "keep[ing] alive for generations to come the spirit of Belford Lawson and to kindle, as he did, another generation of young talented Black men who will gaze upon the Alpha legacy of leadership and service and say, 'we can and we must . . . carry on!'"[26] Not surprisingly, many of the orations by the young Alpha men are calls for racial equality in the United States.

New Negro Alliance

When Lawson left Michigan, he worked for three years as the head football coach and athletic director at Jackson College (today known as Jackson State University), a historically black college in Jackson, Mississippi. While there, he was director of the Teachers Professional Department and a professor of social science. He left and briefly held a teaching position at Morris Brown College, a black institution in Atlanta, Georgia. He was also the head coach of the football team.[27] John Lewis, the college's president, was a Yale University graduate. He helped Lawson gain entry to Yale Law School. Lawson did not graduate, because he did not have the money to complete his education. He went to Washington, DC, and worked for the Supreme Liberty Life Insurance Company, where he was the manager of the "mixed department."[28] Lawson was admitted to Howard University, where he received a law degree in 1932. The next year he opened a law firm with Theodore Moody Berry, a Cincinnati lawyer, who was also an Alpha member.[29]

Charles Hamilton Houston was the dean of Howard School of Law. He believed that the students should emerge as superior professionals committed to making the world better. According to Houston, "A lawyer's either a social engineer or . . . a parasite on society. . . . A social engineer [is] a highly skilled, perceptive, sensitive lawyer who [understands] the Constitution of the United States and [knows] how to explore its uses in the solving of problems of local communities and in bettering conditions of the underprivileged citizens."[30] Houston, sometimes referred to as "the man who killed Jim Crow," played a role in every significant civil rights case from the 1930s to the *Brown v. Board of Education of Topeka* decision in 1954. He used his position at Howard to recruit and groom talented students for the fight against legal segregation. Lawson was one of those students.

In August 1933, John Aubrey Davis, a twenty-one-year-old writer/activist organized a boycott of the white-owned Hamburger Grill, a restaurant in Washington, DC. The diner, located in a black neighborhood—and almost wholly dependent on black patronage—had recently fired three black employees and replaced them with whites. This was during the Great Depression, with roughly 25 percent unemployment nationally, and many others underemployed. Jobs were scarce, and the assumption at the Hamburger Grill—and many other white-owned businesses in the country—was that white people should be given preference when jobs were available, and jobs could be made available by firing black workers.

Davis channeled his anger. He gathered a group of young African Americans who frequented the Hamburger Grill. They stood in front of the grill carrying signs urging fellow community members to boycott the restaurant. The protest produced a quick victory. On the second day of the picketing, the restaurant rehired the three black workers.

The successful protest convinced Davis that racial discrimination was best addressed by street level activism. He discussed the political implications of the Hamburger Grill demonstration and the possibility of similar direct actions with a group of black professionals living in the Washington, DC, area. Among that group were Lawson and Houston, Thurman Dodson, William Hastie, James Nabrit Jr., and Doxey Wilkerson.[31] Davis's discussions with his colleagues convinced him that the success of the picketing and threatened boycott of the Hamburger

Grill could be—and should be—replicated throughout the Washington, DC, area. He was also convinced that these efforts needed to be handled by an organization dedicated to direct "hit them in the wallet" activism.

Davis joined with two others—M. Franklin Thorne, a recent college graduate, and Lawson—to found the New Negro Alliance (NNA). The NNA adopted the then radical slogan "Don't Buy Where You Can't Work." Small groups of black people carried signs with those words—or similar ones— in front of white-owned businesses that refused to hire black employees or only hired them for menial jobs. Some businesses complied with the demands of the NNA, but others refused. These businesses complained that the NNA had no legal right to picket and boycott their businesses, because no one in the Alliance worked at the businesses. In other words, "Nonemployees don't tell us whom to hire or how to run our affairs."

In 1938, the NNA met a challenge from the Sanitary Grocery Company, a Delaware corporation that operated 255 retail grocery, meat, and vegetable stores, a warehouse, and a bakery in Washington, DC, many in African American neighborhoods. The company sought an injunction restraining the NNA and their agents from picketing its stores and engaging in other activities injurious to its business. The case reached the United States Supreme Court.

Lawyers for Sanitary Grocery made several arguments: the NNA was attempting to force the grocery to fire experienced white managerial and sales workers and replace them with inexperienced black employees; the grocery should be free in the selection and control of persons employed by it without interference; the NNA had used the threat of pickets and boycotts—and actual pickets and boycotts—to try to ruin the business done at a specific Sanitary Grocery store, located at 1936 Eleventh Street Northwest; some of the picketers had physically intimated potential customers from entering; the NNA had threatened to use similar "unlawful" acts—meaning the protests themselves and acts of physical coercion—at other Sanitary Grocery stores.

The NNA legal team, led by Lawson, was a Who's Who of civil rights litigators, including Thurmond L. Dodson, Thurgood Marshall, William Hastie, and James M. Nabrit Jr. They denied the allegations made by Sanitary Grocery and claimed that they only sought to have the company, "in the regular course of personnel changes in its retail stores, give employment to negroes as clerks, particularly in stores patronized largely by colored people." They acknowledged that the NNA had threatened the "use of lawful and peaceable persuasion of members of the community to withhold patronage from particular stores" unless the grocery adopted a policy of employing black workers.[32]

The Supreme Court ruled that the alliance had the legal right to picket a business, regardless of whether the picketers worked there. This win strengthened the NNA. *New Negro Alliance v. Sanitary Grocery* became a landmark in the struggle by African Americans against discriminatory hiring practices, and Don't Buy Where You Can't Work groups multiplied throughout the nation. Michele F. Pacifico, an archivist at the National Archives, summarized the importance of the NNA victory:

> The New Negro Alliance's Supreme Court triumph was a victory not only for African Americans in Washington, but for all labor, black and white. Establishing the legal right to picket to protest unfair employment opportunities was considered by many within the Alliance to be the highlight of the group's efforts. Attorneys Hastie and Lawson set precedents for future civil rights cases, including *Brown v. the Board of Education*, by citing economic, demographic, and sociological data to argue that African Americans had both a bonafide dispute and the right to fight to correct discrimination.[33]

Although much of Lawson's fame as a civil rights litigator resulted from his work with *New Negro Alliance v. Sanitary Grocery*, his work on another civil rights case was sufficient to demonstrate his importance to the emerging civil rights movement. He led the legal team that won *Henderson v. United States*, a case that abolished segregation in railroad dining cars. The case began in 1942, when Lawson was general counsel of Alpha Phi Alpha, and ended while he was the fraternity's president. The Alphas provided financial backing for the legal team from the outset.

On May 17, 1942, Elmer W. Henderson, field representative for President Roosevelt's Committee on Fair Employment Practices, boarded a Southern Railway train in Washington, DC, intending to travel to Atlanta and then to Birmingham, Alabama. Henderson was a black man. His job involved investigating alleged violations of an executive order issued by the president on June 25, 1941, prohibiting racial discrimination by defense contractors. But his job title did not protect him from experiencing racial discrimination on the train ride.

On the evening of his travel, while the train was in Virginia, Henderson went to the dining car. It was the practice of the railroad company to set aside two tables near the kitchen for black patrons. However, if whites filled up the dining car before any black people arrived, the two "Negro tables" were given to white diners. When Henderson arrived to eat, the dining car was filled with white people. There was one empty seat at a Negro table—which meant that Henderson, if served, would be eating with white patrons. The dining car steward offered to serve Henderson at a Pullman seat, Henderson refused.[34] Beginning at 5:30 p.m., Henderson made three visits to the dining car. Each time, whites occupied the Negro tables, and each time he was turned away. When the railroad detached the dining car around 9:00 p.m., Henderson still had not eaten."[35]

Henderson was humiliated and angry, shamed in front of white passengers and black waiters. He contacted Lawson, who had a reputation as a formidable civil rights attorney. Lawson filed a complaint with the Interstate Commerce Commission (ICC), charging that Southern Railway had violated Section 3 of the Interstate Commerce Act, which barred subjecting passengers to "any undue or unreasonable prejudice or disadvantage."[36] The ICC acknowledged that Henderson was subjected to undue and unreasonable prejudice and disadvantage; however, it dismissed the incident as a minor affair caused by the bad judgment of an employee. Worse, the commission refused to enter an order regarding future practices on trains.

Henderson appealed to the United States District Court for the District of Maryland. That court ruled that the railroad's general practice, as evidenced by its stated policies in effect on August 6, 1942, violated the Interstate Commerce Act. In response, Southern Railway, in 1946, changed its practice to "accommodate" black passengers. One table with four seats would be reserved for black diners; however, a curtain was to be placed between the white tables and the black table. This arrangement offended Hamilton, Lawson, and civil rights leaders across the nation. Lawson said, "It was as if you were a pig or some kind of animal."[37] The ICC, notorious for its support of Jim Crow regulations, disagreed. Unfortunately for opponents of Jim Crow, a lower court held that the railroad's practice was not unfair. Lawson was convinced that the only good result would come from the Supreme Court.

Henderson and the legal team led by Lawson wanted more than the end of segregation in the railroad dining cars;[38] they wanted the removal of all separate but equal laws and practices in the United States. Lawson argued to the Supreme Court justices that they had a duty to decide the constitutionality of the separate but equal doctrine—and the Henderson case presented a basis for overturning the doctrine, its legal standing, and its practices. Lawson showed a picture of a roped off table, then described the practice as "a remnant of slavery and a badge of inferiority." Lawson told the judges that black people "have lived in the dark night of Jim Crow long enough."[39]

But the Supreme Court would not go that far. The High Court's mandate eliminated the "Negro tables" and curtains on railroads, but the court refused to rule on the separate but equal doctrine. Not surprisingly, later that year, Southern Railway was again accused of segregating black people in its dining cars despite the Supreme Court ruling. Lawson threatened to file a new suit unless the company halted its discriminatory practices.[40] For his part, Lawson was convinced that Jim Crow laws and practices—founded on the separate but equal doctrine—would soon die. In April 1951, Lawson, then president of the Alpha Phi Alpha fraternity, said, "God has spoken to this generation and the dawn is breaking on the muted midnight of segregation as it rises in the dust of its last hours."[41] In the audience were hundreds of Alpha members eager to help. Lawson predicted the end of racial segregation and Jim Crow, "We are facing the final destruction of the monster 'separate but equal' and no man, no nation, no race can stand in the way of the ultimate triumph of God's word."[42]

He was right. Three years later, the United States Supreme Court decided *Brown v. Board of Education of Topeka*, which declared state laws establishing separate public schools for black and white students to be unconstitutional—and by extension ruled that de jure racial segregation was a violation of the Equal Protection Clause of the Fourteenth Amendment to the United States Constitution. *Henderson v. United States* was one of several cases that laid the foundation for the Brown decision.

Relationships

Marjorie M. McKenzie was one of the attorneys who assisted with *Henderson v. United States*. She earned a bachelor's degree from the University of Michigan in 1933. The following year she earned a certificate in social work from that university. After graduation, she attended the Robert H. Terrell School of Law, in Washington, DC. She earned her law degree and passed the District of Columbia bar examination in 1939. While attending law school, she met Lawson, who by the late 1930s was treated as a celebrity in national black newspapers. The gossip section of the *Pittsburgh Courier* suggested that Lawson and McKenzie might marry.

> Well! It was lovely, anyway. Pretties here . . . pretties there! Marjorie McKenzie was here from Dee Cee . . . looking lovely. And Belford Lawson, too . . . and they DO say this is going to be a match some of these near days.[43]

The columnist was right. The couple married the next year, and she joined his law firm. Together and individually, they greatly impacted this nation. Belford Lawson lived a life of *firsts*—the first African American to win a case before the United States Supreme Court, address the Democratic National Convention, serve as a board member of Madison National Bank in the nation's capital, and be elected as president of the Young Men's Christian Association (YMCA). Marjorie McKenzie Lawson also had an impressive career. She was a columnist for the *Pittsburgh Courier* from 1941 to 1955, when it was arguably the most influential black newspaper

The Lawsons at home in 1952.

in the country. From 1943 to 1946, she served as assistant director (and then director) of the Division of Review and Analysis of the President's Commission on Fair Employment Practices. After being passed over for another federal position—which was awarded to a white male graduate from an Ivy League law school—she returned to law school, earning a JD from Columbia University. In 1959, she was named to the Federal Housing Administration's Industry Advisory Committee on Valuation, becoming its only African American member and second woman member. In 1961, President Kennedy appointed her to the Committee on Equal Employment Opportunity. The next year, he appointed her to the Juvenile Court, the first black woman appointed to this position by a president. She remained in that position until 1965, the year that President Lyndon B. Johnson appointed her United States representative to the United Nations Economic and Social Council.[44]

The Lawsons played a vital role in John F. Kennedy's presidential drive in 1960.[45] Belford met Kennedy in 1952, when both attended the Democratic National Convention in Chicago. Lawson described his early contacts with then senator Kennedy as "purely social." Four years later, the relationship deepened.

Belford Lawson is shown advising John F. Kennedy, February 4, 1960.

> Then in 1956 when he was a candidate for the vice presidency, I met him on the floor of the Convention. I told him I was a delegate to the Convention from the District of Columbia and my delegation was for [Estes] Kefauver, but I was holding out for him because I had been studying his record and admired him. He then invited me to his office in the Senate. Shortly thereafter I went, and we got well acquainted. I recall [Theodore C.] Ted Sorensen and [Timothy J.] Ted Reardon were there, and we talked generally about his future. He was up for reelection in 1958, and he wanted to know whom I knew in Boston. I told him I knew a good number of people, having a summer place at Martha's Vineyard. In that connection over the years I knew a lot of people in New England—friends and fraternity brothers of mine. He said he would like us to help him in his 58 campaign for the Senate.[46]

In their meetings, Kennedy "spelled out his hopes and plans for the country and for himself," and Lawson told the young Senator that "he would be the first Catholic president of the United States."[47] From 1956 on, the Lawsons were friends with and advisors to Kennedy, who was virtually unknown to most black people—and not trusted by the prominent black people who did know him. Today, Kennedy is viewed as a champion for civil rights; however, when Lawson first met Kennedy, the young senator was more concerned with pragmatic politics than with protecting the civil rights of black people. Earl Ofari Hutchinson, a political analyst, offered this assessment:

> In the decade before he won the White House, Kennedy said almost nothing about civil rights. In 1957, as a senator he voted against the 1957 civil rights bill. His opposition has been spun two ways: one cynical, one charitable. The cynical spin is he opposed it to appease Southern Democrats because he had an eye on a presidential run in 1960. The charitable spin is that he thought the bill was weak and ineffectual. Three years later though he ignored the angry shouts from Southern Democrats and lobbied for a forceful civil rights plank in the Democratic Party's 1960 platform.[48]

The Lawsons were among the first influential African Americans to campaign for Kennedy, and that campaigning included making speeches and introducing Kennedy to influential black people—Roy Wilkins, Benjamin Mays, Samuel D. Proctor, Theodore Berry, Sam Westerfield, and many others. Lawson was an admirer of John Johnson, the publisher of *Jet* and *Ebony* magazines, whose publications had run articles critical of Kennedy. Lawson arranged a brunch at Kennedy's house in Georgetown. The guests included Johnson. Kennedy, through force of his personality and arguments, convinced Johnson that he was serious about racial justice. The treatment of Kennedy in Johnson's publications went from negative to neutral to favorable.

Even though Kennedy had courted southern politicians—many of whom were staunch segregationists—as the presidential campaign neared he more closely aligned himself with African American individuals and organizations. Lawson helped move him in that direction. For example, in 1959, four or five hundred practitioners of the Howard University Medical Association met on that campus. They invited Kennedy to address their organization. He, in turn, asked Lawson if he should honor the invitation. Lawson said yes. Kennedy delivered the talk after being introduced to the audience by Lawson. Years later, Lawson remembered that Kennedy "received a tremendous ovation."[49]

> I think I can say with propriety and with truth that the great majority of Negro leaders—and a lot of white people came to support Kennedy because of what my wife and I—mainly my wife, because she gave it more time—did in support of Kennedy.[50]

On October 26, 1960, Martin Luther King Jr. was arrested in Georgia during a sit-in, transferred to a maximum-security prison, and sentenced to four months on a chain gang.[51] Coretta, his wife, worried that her husband would be locked away—or beaten and killed. Kennedy and Richard Nixon were locked in a tight campaign. Nixon considered telephoning Mrs. King to offer words of sympathy but decided against it, because his advisors warned that the call might alienate white voters in the South. Kennedy called her. It may have come from his sense of moral duty. It may have been a symbolic act calculated to gain political favor with black voters. Whatever the motivation, when word got out—mainly through black newspapers—that Kennedy had called the worried (and pregnant) Mrs. King to express his sympathy and concern about her husband's prison confinement, it gained him a measure of respect in black America.

Robert Kennedy, the United States attorney general and John's brother, interceded with the Georgia authorities to orchestrate King's release. King's father, a lifelong Republican, was so moved by the actions of John and Robert Kennedy that he stated, "I've got all my votes and I've got a suitcase, and I'm going to take them up there and dump them in his [Kennedy's] lap," meaning he would use his influence to help John Kennedy win the election.[52]

Kennedy's reputation as a civil rights champion was also enhanced by a televised address that he gave on June 11, 1963. Alabama governor George Wallace had refused to allow "two clearly qualified young Alabama residents who happen to have been born Negro" to be admitted to the University of Alabama. Kennedy federalized the Alabama National Guard to make sure that no one—including Wallace—could block the paths of the black students as they entered campus buildings. In a blunt and eloquent address, Kennedy argued that this country was founded on the principle that all men are created equal, but first-class citizenship was denied to black people:

> The heart of the question is whether all Americans are to be afforded equal rights and equal opportunities, whether we are going to treat our fellow Americans as we want to be treated. If an American, because his skin is dark, cannot eat lunch in a restaurant open to the public, if he cannot send his children to the best public school available, if he cannot vote for the public officials who will represent

him, if, in short, he cannot enjoy the full and free life which all of us want, then who among us would be content to have the color of his skin changed and stand in his place? Who among us would then be content with the counsels of patience and delay? One hundred years of delay have passed since President Lincoln freed the slaves, yet their heirs, their grandsons, are not fully free. They are not yet freed from the bonds of injustice. They are not yet freed from social and economic oppression. And this Nation, for all its hopes and all its boasts, will not be fully free until all its citizens are free. We preach freedom around the world, and we mean it, and we cherish our freedom here at home, but are we to say to the world, and much more importantly, to each other that this is the land of the free except for the Negroes; that we have no second-class citizens except Negroes; that we have no class or caste system, no ghettoes, no master race except with respect to Negroes? Now the time has come for this Nation to fulfill its promise.[53]

Kennedy ended his address by promising to ask Congress to enact legislation protecting voting rights, legal standing, educational opportunities, and access to public facilities for all Americans. He did not live to see that legislation pass; he was assassinated on November 22, 1963, in a presidential motorcade, in Dallas, Texas. On July 2, 1964, Lyndon B. Johnson, Kennedy's successor as president, signed into law the Civil Rights Act of 1964, which banned discrimination based on race, color, religion, sex, or national origin.

There were other politicians influenced by Lawson, most notably Edward W. Brooke. In 1962, Brooke was elected attorney general of Massachusetts, making him the first African American to hold that position in any state. His most significant political achievement came in 1966, when he defeated former governor Endicott Peabody to become the first African American elected to the United States Senate since Reconstruction. As a senator, Brooke coauthored the 1968 Fair Housing Act, which prohibited discrimination in housing.[54] He served two terms. Lawson was a friend and mentor to Brooke. Although they were members of different political parties (Lawson, Democrat, Brooke, Republican), Lawson campaigned for Brooke. They were longtime friends, and the younger Brooke affectionately referred to his mentor as grandfather.[55] Among Lawson's other protégés were Ernest Morial, who became mayor

This is one of the pens used by President Lyndon B. Johnson to sign the Civil Rights Act of 1964 into law. The pen is displayed in the Jim Crow Museum at Ferris State University.

of New Orleans and chairman of the United States Conference of Mayors, and David Grant, a distinguished St. Louis lawyer and civil rights leader, who was active in Democratic politics and eventually served as president of the St. Louis National Association for the Advancement of Colored People (NAACP).[56]

The relationship between Belford Lawson and Thurgood Marshall was not as amicable; indeed, at times it was antagonistic. Lawson and Marshall were—to use the parlance of the time—*race men*: public figures who promote the interests of black people and "seek remedy for harms to the black body caused by the gospel and practice of white supremacy."[57] They were members of Alpha Phi Alpha when that fraternity was a leading civil rights organization. They were graduates of the Howard School of Law, trained and mentored by Charles Hamilton Houston. Lawson, seven years Marshall's senior, received his JD in 1932; Marshall was graduated the next year. They were skilled, tough attorneys who saw the federal courts as the primary vehicle to attack Jim Crow laws and customs. They had much in common and shared overlapping professional and social circles, but any chance for a friendship ended with the case of *Murray v. Pearson*.

A number of influential figures attended a 1951 civil liberties dinner—from left to right: Adam Clayton Powell, Raymond Pace Alexander, Thurgood Marshall, Sadie T.M. Alexander, Belford Lawson, Jawn A. Sandifer, and Channing H. Tobias.

Donald Gaines Murray was a talented student from an influential Baltimore family. In 1934, Murray, the grandson of A.L. Gaines, a well-known African Methodist bishop, was awarded the John Franklin Genung Prize for excellence in prose at Amherst College.[58] Later that year, he was graduated with a Bachelor of Arts degree. His academic transcript showed high marks. In January 1935, Murray applied for admission to the University of Maryland School of Law. His application was rejected. The university did not admit black students. He appealed to the university's board of regents. Again, he was turned away. Although Murray was not a member, the Alpha Phi Alpha fraternity hired Lawson to represent him.

Lawson was excited. He called Houston to inform him that Murray would be a perfect test for undermining the university's ban on black students. Houston contacted Marshall, told him that he should meet with Lawson—but not to make any promises. Marshall did not meet with Lawson. Instead, he decided that he, with the help of Houston, would try the case. Juan Williams, one of Marshall's biographers, wrote:

> Marshall now saw his chance to take revenge for the hurt he felt when he discovered his home state law school was closed to him. He had held the anger for years, later saying that the first thing he wanted to do after he got out of Howard was "get even with Maryland for not letting me go to its law school." When Marshall heard through the grapevine that some lawyers in Washington

were thinking about suing the law school, he got upset and wrote to Houston that he wanted to be the first to file suit. He could not bear to allow any other lawyer to take the lead on the case.[59]

Houston and Marshall met with Murray and convinced him that they, with the resources of the national NAACP, had a better chance for victory—replacing Lawson as the lead attorney. At trial, the NAACP attorneys argued that the university's practice of barring black students was unconstitutional, and that since the state of Maryland did not provide a comparable law school—*separate but equal*—for black people, Murray should be allowed to attend the white university. The judge issued a writ of mandamus ordering Raymond A. Pearson, president of the university, to admit Murray. The ruling was appealed to Maryland's highest court, the Court of Appeals, which affirmed the lower court's rulings on January 15, 1936. Murray was admitted to the University of Maryland School of Law.

Although Houston did much of the work, *Murray v. Pearson* helped launch the career of Thurgood Marshall. In the years that followed, Lawson would work with Marshall (and Houston) on civil rights initiatives, including cases that attacked Jim Crow. However, Lawson would never forgive the slight.

A Commitment to Social Justice

The struggle for social justice popularly referred to as the civil rights movement is often seen as a 1950s and 1960s occurrence. This, of course, ignores the efforts of black people like Belford Lawson and the New Negro Alliance, who picketed and boycotted white stores to combat racial discrimination—when Martin Luther King Jr. was still a student at Yonge Street Elementary School. One can debate when the American civil rights movement began (and ended), but there is no doubt that the social justice work done in the 1930s and 1940s was beneficial in its own right—and laid a foundation for the civil rights activities that came later.

Lawson worked with many civil rights leaders, including Martin Luther King Jr. and the bus boycott leaders in Montgomery, whom he compared to Mohandas Gandhi "and other mystics who won victories without firing a shot."[60] Early in his career, he too walked with picket signs, demanding that black people be treated fairly and be given opportunities to work in jobs that paid a living wage. In the 1930s, he marched with the New Negro Alliance to help hundreds of well-qualified black people gain

Belford Lawson shown conversing with Martin Luther King Jr. in 1967.

positions of respect in "not only the community stores but the larger mercantile establishments as well."[61]

Lawson had interactions (and often friendships) with many of the civil rights leaders who show up in history books, including Bayard Rustin, Adam Clayton Powell, Paul Robeson, Samuel D. Proctor, and W.E.B. Du Bois. In 1951, Du Bois, then eighty-three years old, was indicted, arrested, and arraigned in federal court on trumped up charges of being an agent of the Soviet Union—presumably because he circulated a petition protesting nuclear weapons. At Du Bois's birthday party, which doubled as a benefit and a rousing demonstration for civil rights, Lawson made a "fighting speech" on Du Bois's behalf.[62]

His advocacy on behalf of Du Bois was predictable; Lawson had a strong commitment to social justice. He knew that Du Bois was being mistreated by the federal government, and he would not stand for it. In 1956, he was a delegate from Washington, DC, to the Democratic Party Convention. Lawson was on the party's Platform Committee. He pushed his Democratic colleagues to adopt a platform that repudiated Jim Crow thinking and practices. This stance put him in opposition to many southern politicians, including George Bell Timmerman Jr., who served as governor of South Carolina from 1955 to 1959. Lawson challenged Timmerman, who said that "catering to the 'Nigras' was going to lose the election for the Democrats and that segregation was the last [and best] of all possible systems for Negroes and whites in the South."[63] Lawson did not back down.

Lawson's commitment to making the world better extended beyond his legal and political efforts. He served on the boards of numerous organizations, including the American Red Cross. He was a vice chairman of the United Negro College Fund. He also served as president of the board of directors of the YMCA of metropolitan Washington, DC, and later became the national president of that organization.[64] In a resolution given to him by the Council of the District of Columbia are these words:

> Belford V. Lawson, Jr., acquired a national reputation as a brilliant and skilled trial advocate who was a relentless foe of racial and social injustice . . . a charismatic person, gifted in elocution and blessed with wit, who walked among the mighty and noble, but was equally at home with the meek and humble.[65]

The young men who came from Hampton to and through Ferris were born and lived during the Jim Crow period. Unlike many of them, Lawson outlived Jim Crow: he died on February 23, 1985. In the late 1940s, he chastised white southerners who opposed President Truman's civil rights program as people who were "educated wrong," adding, "In America, we preach a creed of equality, but practice a code of white supremacy."[66] Although he was a strong and persistent opponent of Jim Crow era attitudes and practices (and their contemporary expressions), he never gave up on America. Lawson believed that the "United States has a historical debt to Negroes to help them make economic and social gains," and he believed that this country—with the urging and hard work of black people, would repay that debt.[67]

Percival L. Prattis painted by Diane Cleland, 2017.

It is our duty to read some Negro newspaper. There are
Two in this town, read one or the other of them. Not
because you may be supporting a Negro editor but due
to the fact that you are a Negro with Race Pride.

—*Negro Star*

Negro Star (Wichita, KS), November 11, 1921, 4. The *Negro Star* was an African American newspaper created by Hollie T. Sims that was published from 1908 to 1953. The paper was founded
in Greenwood, Mississippi, but Sims was harassed by the city sheriff and other whites after
he wrote a tribute to black soldiers serving during World War I. To avoid the racial hostility,
he moved the newspaper to Wichita, Kansas, in 1919.

Race News: African American Journalists

Percival Leroy Prattis was a pioneering journalist, influential newspaper executive, and nationally recognized civil rights leader. He was the city editor of the *Chicago Defender* when it was the nation's leading African American weekly newspaper. Later, he spent thirty years at the *Pittsburgh Courier*, another prominent black paper. In 1947, as a representative of *Our World* magazine, he became the first African American news correspondent to be admitted to the United States House and Senate press galleries. Prattis rivals Belford Lawson as the most accomplished of the Hampton students who came to Ferris.

He was born on April 27, 1895, in Philadelphia, Pennsylvania, to Alexander and Ella (Spraggins) Prattis. He began his education at the Christiansburg Industrial Institute in Cambria (now Christiansburg), Virginia. The school was founded by Charles S. Schaeffer, a Union soldier and Baptist minister. Working for the Freedmen's Bureau, Schaeffer came to Christiansburg in 1866 and taught former slaves in a rented house. In 1870, the Friends Freedmen's Association, a Quaker group, became the main financial backers of the school.[1] In the 1880s, Schaeffer turned over control of the school to a completely African American staff.[2] Booker T. Washington became an adviser to the Christiansburg Institute in 1896. Soon after that, the school changed its curriculum to align it with those at Tuskegee and Hampton. Prattis remained at Christiansburg for four years, literally working his way through school—milking cows at the school's dairy farm during the day and attending classes at night. He was valedictorian of his class.

Prattis left Christiansburg on the night of the day that he was graduated, taking an all-night train across the state. He was seventeen years old and on his way to Hampton Institute. He would later write: "As I catnapped through the night, I felt like I was riding in the sky—I was going to the great Booker T. Washington school, the school which motivated him to found Tuskegee Institute."[3] Christiansburg and Hampton were both black schools with a focus on practical education, but the young Prattis quickly noticed differences:

> At Hampton, the picture was different from Christiansburg. Hampton was much larger, with many more impressive buildings. It was like a small town. There were more students than at Christiansburg. The students were black and red, or Negroes and Indians. As nearly as I can recall, not more than three of the academic teachers were Negroes. Some of the teachers of trades were white. The head of the Agricultural department was a white graduate of Pennsylvania State College. All of the white teachers, male and female seemed to have been graduates from northern colleges and universities. They were affable, friendly and devoted to their responsibilities as servants for the students.[4]

Without much money, Prattis had to work his way through Hampton— he worked in the institute's dairy farm for three years. Because of this work, he was placed in the agricultural program (which took three years to complete). He wanted to enroll in college preparatory courses, but the school did not offer many, and the ones that were offered conflicted with the requirements of his program. Prattis spent many hours searching for his life's path. His experiences at Christiansburg and Hampton were more training than education—training to accept life as a farmer, albeit one able to teach others to farm. He wanted something different.

> I had to admit that I did not want to spend my life behind a plow or milking a cow. I had no prejudice against farming. Farming was the basis of civilization in Egypt and Samaria thousands of years ago. Even so, I never had the feeling that I could make good, be successful as a farmer.[5]

Some of his classmates told him about a school in Michigan, where a black man could take college preparatory courses. He did not have the money for tuition. So, in 1915, the year after graduating from Hampton,

Percival Prattis (top row, second from left) was a member of the 1917 Wednesday night debate club.

Prattis took a job as "poultry master"—actually a foreman—at Shellbanks farm, an auxiliary of Hampton.[6] In the fall of 1916, he enrolled at Ferris Institute to "pick up the academic subjects that Hampton's vocational program had not provided."[7] Although battered by a difficult Michigan winter—"temperatures hovering around 40 degrees below zero"—Prattis found his year at Ferris to be rewarding.

> Ferris Institute was really great. It was an acknowledged "cram" school. Everybody worked hard, including the teachers. If you needed extra tutoring, the teachers gave it to you without extra cost. Our saint, of course, was Woodbridge N. Ferris, the white-haired founder of the school who later became Governor of Michigan.[8]

Today, the word *cram* has a slightly negative connotation, meaning, to prepare hastily for an examination. When Prattis referred to Ferris as a cram school, he meant that the college preparatory program offered short intensive courses. And Prattis wanted to delve into as much learning as he could squeeze into an academic year.

> I was at Ferris from September 1916, until June 1917. During that period, practically ten months, I covered the following courses: two

years of French, two years of Latin, algebra, plane geometry, trigonometry, rhetoric, physiography and spelling. According to present-
day grading, I made A's [above 90] in all subjects but trigonometry
in which I made 85. . . . It would be a grave sort of indifference for
me to fail to name some of the teachers who went out of their way
to help me. Among them were Mr. Masselink, vice president, who
taught in the college preparatory department; Mr. Carlisle regarded
as the "biggest little man in the state"; and Mr. St. Peter who, it
was reputed, could do anything with electricity: and carried tables
for mathematics in his head. These men made me feel like I had a
chance in life. So did many of the students.[9]

This is a poignant and revealing testimony. At a time when the
South—and other parts of the country—still had racial hierarchies, Prattis
felt welcomed at Ferris. He was involved with the Wednesday night debate
club and the interscholastic debate team. He was also selected as one of
the editors for the yearbook. He graduated from the college preparatory
program in 1917.[10] He planned to enter law school, but those plans were
interrupted when he was "called up to the army."

I was inducted in August, 1918, and sent to Camp Sherman,
Chillicothe, Ohio. The going was not rough once we reached camp.
Our training was a bit peculiar. My first training was in the peeling
of potatoes. I was given a stool to sit on outside the camp kitchen
and put on K.P. [kitchen police] duty. I did nothing but peel potatoes
all morning. However, after lunch I would stroll up to the company
office to see if anybody was using the typewriter.[11]

One can dispute the reasons that the United States joined World War
I, but there is no arguing that a popular narrative was that the United
States was fighting for its liberty and attempting to spread democracy.
Although many black Americans rightly saw the hypocrisy in this narrative, they hoped that if they fought—and fought bravely—when they
returned to this country they would be granted the basic rights denied
to them. Hollis Burke Frissell, the principal of Hampton Institute, sent
letters to Hampton graduates calling on them to "stand shoulder to shoulder" with all Americans to "rally to the defense of the nation."[12] Whether
influenced by Frissell's letters or not—Hampton graduates joined thousands of other black men in "the war to end all wars." They saw military

service, a significant civic obligation, as the way for them to be treated as first-class citizens.

Unfortunately, black soldiers could not escape Jim Crow. Black people were not allowed to serve in the marines and the navy confined them to mess duty on ships. Most black soldiers in the army received inadequate training and served in labor battalions. Prattis summed it up this way:

> There were many of these [black] regiments. Ours was known as the 813th Pioneer Infantry Regiment. How easy it is to delude with words! We were not really going to France to fight, although some of us might carry. We were being shipped over there to work, to do the hard and dirty work. All except me.[13]

His unit was made up of black enlisted personnel and junior officers, supervised by white senior officers. The unit was responsible for filling shell holes, helping with road construction (often under fire), clearing battlegrounds, and reburying bodies that had been hurriedly buried at the time of their death.

> We were all members of the 813th Pioneer Infantry. Uncle had not planned for us to do anything new or different in France. We had worked with our hands in the good old U.S.A. and Uncle planned to put our hands to work in France. Pioneer Infantry meant "pioneer work" or "pioneer labor." For everybody but me.[14]

A white colonel from Alabama pulled Prattis away from the other black soldiers. He had seen him using a typewriter. He asked Prattis about his schooling. Prattis told him about his experiences at Christiansburg, Hampton, and Ferris. He talked about the courses that he had taken. When the questioning concluded, Prattis was promoted to a sergeant major and told he would work behind a typewriter—over black privates, corporals, sergeants, and first sergeants. Prattis was pleased. "Man, that was something—a private one day and a sergeant major the next. My weapon from that point on was a typewriter—and I had rank."[15] He never carried a pistol or rifle.

He was stationed in France from September 15, 1918, to July 13, 1919, and was honorably discharged from his duties on July 23, 1919. His military service gave him the beginnings of a global perspective, which served him well in future reporting from and about Europe, Africa, and Asia.[16] It also inflamed in him an even greater dislike of Jim Crow racism.

After returning from the war, Prattis settled in Grand Rapids, Michigan. He knew the city well. It was only fifty miles from Big Rapids, and he had spent several months there before reporting for military duty. He had worked first in a barbershop—"to keep a barber shop clean and to shine the shoes of customers"—then later as a bellboy in the Pantlind Hotel.[17] Although he had been a sergeant major, after returning to the country, he still only found menial labor: this time work as a waiter at the Pantlind Hotel.

While working at the hotel, Prattis was asked to substitute for Roscoe Conkling Simmons, a celebrated orator who had been scheduled to speak at a fundraising dinner for the Red Cross. This brought Prattis—and his talents—to the attention of the black community in Grand Rapids. Around that time, he also joined with his friend George Smith to begin a weekly newspaper targeted to the local black population. Smith, a printer and the secretary of the local National Association for the Advancement of Colored People (NAACP), had access to printing equipment but needed someone to function as editor and reporter. He asked Prattis to join him. Prattis was flattered but uncertain.

> I agreed with hesitation. I knew nothing about journalism. My real love was mathematics and I could work all night on a single math problem. In mathematics, you know there is a "right" answer but in writing—poetry, novels, news stories—it is hard to say for sure when, if ever, you have arrived at the correct answer.[18]

Thus began Prattis's career as a journalist and executive. The *Michigan State News* became the first African American newspaper in Grand Rapids.[19] The paper's motto was "Michigan's Race Paper," and it was unapologetically an opponent of Jim Crow laws and practices. Smith was an NAACP officer; therefore, the *Michigan State News* highlighted the work of that organization. For example, an early edition of the newspaper gave extensive coverage to the visit of Walter White, national secretary of the NAACP, to Kalamazoo and Lansing.[20] Randall Jelks, a historian, summarized the relationship between the newspaper and the local African American community:

> The *Michigan State News* bolstered the work of the NAACP and kept the small African American community in Grand Rapids informed about civil rights matters nationwide. The paper and the work of

the national NAACP provided the encouragement that some in the African American community needed in their own battle with Jim Crow.[21]

Prattis worked for the *Michigan State News* when he was not required to be at the hotel, and he must have enjoyed it, because he worked without pay. His time at the newspaper awoke in him a love of journalism and a belief that papers run by black people could be tools of activism. He had not been naive about race relations—some of his schooling was in the South, and he served in a segregated army—but his time spent at the *Michigan State News* gave him a deeper understanding of racism and a vehicle for addressing racial injustice.

He worked at the *Michigan State News* for two years and likely would have stayed longer, but an incident at his paying job provided him the impetus to leave Grand Rapids. White waitresses at the Pantlind Hotel called one of the black waiters a nigger. The black waiters caucused and decided to make a demand of the hotel managers: the white women should be fired. If the women were not fired all the men—thirty black men— agreed that they would quit en masse. This did not turn out well for Prattis.

> I was too wet behind the ears to realize that men with families who were probably paying for their homes and furniture, would take some second thoughts before giving up their jobs and jeopardizing the welfare of their families. The manager would not fire the girls. When the time came to quit, as we had threatened, only three out of thirty quit. I was among the three. That was why, in January of 1921, I found myself in Chicago completely alone.[22]

He arrived in Chicago without money. Once again, he found employment as a waiter. Shortly thereafter, he was introduced to Robert Sengstacke Abbott, founder and publisher of the *Chicago Defender*.[23] Abbott was drawn to Prattis. Both men had attended Hampton Institute—and both believed that a black-run newspaper could be a powerful tool in the fight against racial injustice. A month after taking a staff job on the *Defender*, Prattis was promoted to city editor, a position he held for two years. Prattis wrote articles and features under his name and under the pen name Roger Didier.

If Prattis's activism was awakened at the *Michigan State News*, it was fed at the *Chicago Defender*, one of the loudest voices encouraging black people to leave the Jim Crow South. *The Defender* published editorials, cartoons, and articles—even job listings and train schedules—to persuade African Americans to move to northern cities. Under the leadership of Abbott, the *Defender* reported the news that mattered to African Americans—for example, coverage of the riots of 1919—and campaigned for anti-lynching legislation, fair housing policies, and the integration of major professional sports leagues. The newspaper was an uncompromising foe of Jim Crow. It seemed like Prattis had found his professional home, but an "unfortunate disagreement," as he put it, with Abbott led Prattis to resign from the newspaper.[24]

Prattis was not out of work very long; in May 1923, he landed a position with the Associated Negro Press (ANP), founded and led by Claude A. Barnett, a graduate of Tuskegee Institute and an admirer of Booker T. Washington. In 1913, Barnett sold advertisements and photographs to black newspapers. He soon realized that these newspapers lacked reporters. In 1919, he created the Chicago-based ANP, which provided black newspapers with stories, commentaries, and featured essays that focused on the black experience, including black people in African countries.[25] Prattis and Barnett also created the National News Gravure, a photogravure supplement that the ANP designed for distribution by black newspapers.[26]

Although primarily a news-sharing operation, Barnett wanted the ANP to also be a source for news coverage. Prattis served as the ANP's city editor, and he worked as a reporter. He traveled on assignment and reported on domestic and international stories. In 1930, Prattis accompanied the Special Committee for the Study of Education in Haiti, headed by Robert R. Moton, president of Tuskegee Institute. The State Department recognized him as an accredited journalist and paid his travel expenses, as if he were a member of the commission. While in Haiti, he addressed several groups of local journalists. His experience in Haiti led him to call for more friendly relations between black Americans and Haitians. When Prattis left in 1935, the ANP served over two hundred newspapers and magazines across the United States.

After a ten-week stint as city editor of the *Amsterdam News* in Harlem, in 1936, he joined the *Pittsburgh Courier*, which had eclipsed the *Chicago Defender* as the most influential black newspaper in the country, with a circulation of over 250,000. He served as city editor until 1940, executive editor until 1956, editor-in-chief until 1961, and finally as associate publisher and treasurer until 1963.[27]

A collage of Percival Prattis columns from the *Pittsburgh Courier*

The Black Journalist

Through much of the Jim Crow era, white newspapers across the nation portrayed black people as childlike buffoons, exotic savages, or dangerous cultural parasites. These portrayals reflected and shaped attitudes toward black people. It was common to find newspapers carrying supposedly humorous yarns about "ignorant darkies"—and, more consequently, articles about "nigger brutes" or "negro brutes" accused of murdering white men and raping white women.

The newspaper offices where racialized stories were written were filled with white men—and, in some cases, white women. Black journalists were often dismissed as sloppy amateurs. White newspaper executives did not hire black journalists until the 1960s—mainly in response to the racial turmoil gripping the nation—and by that time Prattis had retired. In a 1975 interview, a decade after retiring, he said, "There are jobs opening up for Negroes now that weren't open when I was coming along," he said, adding, "Sometimes I wish I were starting all over again so I could take advantage of some of these opportunities."[28]

Had he been a white man during the time he lived—or a black man today—it is likely that Prattis would have had a distinguished career at a white newspaper. But a black journalist plying his or her trade during the Jim Crow period only found work with black newspapers. "I was on social terms with a lot of white editors and publishers," he said, "but none of them would have dreamed of hiring me."[29] By spending his career at the *Chicago Defender* and the *Pittsburgh Courier*, he was empowered to fight against racial segregation and other forms of racial injustice.

During the Jim Crow period, black newspapers were unabashedly pro-black, agitating for social justice *and* black empowerment. They could do this—indeed, were expected to do this by the African American community—because they were not dependent on whites for their existence. Black people owned the newspapers, and black people were the primary consumers of the newspapers. The black press had freedom that most black institutions did not have, and with that freedom came responsibility.[30] In a 1946 speech, Prattis portrayed the black press as an agent for social change and the black reporter as a fighting partisan.

> In enumerating the functions of the Negro press, I place first the promotion of the welfare of Negroes and the fighting of their battles. The first Negro newspaper in 1827 was born in protest against slavery. Every Negro newspaper published during the 19th century accepted the challenge either to fight slavery or the restrictions which limited the Negro's development as a free man or a first-class citizen. The chief function of the Negro newspaper, along with other forces in Negro life, is to fight for first-class citizenship and full growth for Negroes.[31]

Prattis was a prolific writer for many years. He wrote about many topics, but he rarely went more than a week or two without writing about the evils of racial segregation. He wanted his readers to understand that racial segregation injured black people in profound ways.

> Someday a sociologist will set himself to the task of assessing what segregation has cost the Negro in the United States in terms of retarded development. He will bill the American people for what they owe the American Negro, not only for required toil during 250 years of slavery, but also for the cultural lag of which the Negro is the handicapped victim. It will be discovered that the Negro's alleged backwardness is their fault, not his. Segregation will be exposed as the evil system which can and does retard the Negro. It will also be learned that the deadly effect of segregation is impartial, that it stunts the growth of any group, regardless of race or color.[32]

Whites, argued Prattis, justified segregation by claiming that black people were inferior—and the supposed inferiority of black people was used to justify discriminating against them. Black people had the potential to achieve as much as white people, but racial segregation—and the beliefs that propped it—made black achievement difficult. Black people had to realize their potential *despite* racial segregation.

> Segregation, imposed from without, is the rigid determinant of the Negro's status in the United States. The kind of segregation of which the Negro is a victim not only stigmatizes him. It does more. It sets him off as inferior and unwanted. It prevents his natural, normal development and makes it impossible for him to keep up with the advances of other elements of the population. It imprisons him in a condition where, even were he superior, only the factor of time is needed to reduce him to an inferior.[33]

Prattis lived most of his life during a time when the United States, primarily but not exclusively the South, operated a racial caste system. Under this system, all whites were considered superior to all blacks in all ways that mattered. This system was supported by and manifested in major societal institutions: government, schools, economy, family, religion, criminal justice, and media. To live as a black person during the Jim Crow period was to be set apart. In his writings, Prattis critiqued the harmful consequences of racial segregation, while simultaneously praising the efforts of black people.

> In spite of segregation, individual Negroes by the scores and hundreds, have attained heights which have marked them as distinguished participants in and contributors to the common culture of America. But the great body of Negroes, blindly and vainly seeking to orient themselves in the general culture, has failed to find footing or rootage. Hemmed in and checked by segregation, they flounder futilely inside cultural concentration camps just as grown-up children do.[34]

In Prattis's view, the United States, by practicing white supremacy, damaged black Americans; nevertheless, black people were responsible for their futures. He was critical of black people who did not take advantage of hard-won civil rights victories by studying, working hard, and being good citizens. He blended the self-help approach of Booker

Collage of images from publications featuring Percival Prattis

T. Washington and the political agitation of W.E.B. Du Bois. Moreover, though he believed that Martin Luther King Jr.'s nonviolent demonstrations were doomed to fail—not enough black people in the country to make it work—he embraced King's notion of a Beloved Community. On the eve of the signing of the 1964 Civil Rights Act, Prattis said:

> Actually, we need one more organization, a sort of National Association for the Advancement of All People—NAAAP. We need such an organization, one that can put in overtime without over-time pay, to build bridges of love, understanding and patriotism so that we can trod the highways that lead to the hearts of men. Now that we have the law, we can start the drive to win men's hearts.[35]

Historical Figure

In 1925, while in Chicago and working for the *Chicago Defender*, Prattis founded *Heebie Jeebies*, the first known black newsmagazine in the United States.[36] There would not be another black newsmagazine until John Johnson's *Ebony*, which appeared in 1945.[37] *Heebie Jeebies* has historical value; however, it did not have the societal impact that one finds in other Prattis activities and projects.

In 1941, the *Pittsburgh Courier* published a series of exposés written by Prattis, describing the brutal treatment of African American soldiers by white military police. Prattis got his information firsthand, by traveling to military bases. The articles angered military post officials, especially those based in the South. There were calls for Prattis to be investigated, presumably for treason. The War Department demanded that the FBI intensify ongoing investigations of the *Courier* and other African American newspapers. The FBI responded to the War Department on November 29, 1941, stating that its investigation failed to show cause for the indictment of the *Courier*.[38]

Prattis was aware that black people who served in the military were segregated, relegated to menial labor, and subjected to verbal and physical abuse. Like others at the *Pittsburgh Courier* and at black newspapers across the North, he believed that the black press had the responsibility to write about the mistreatment of black people in the armed services. Prattis was one of the architects of the Double V for Victory campaign—to promote the fight against fascism abroad and racial discrimination at home. The genesis of the campaign was a letter sent to the *Courier* by James G. Thompson, eloquently demanding that African Americans who risk their lives fighting for the United States should be treated as first-class citizens when they returned from the battlefields.

> Being an American of dark complexion and some 26 years, these questions flash through my mind! "Should I sacrifice my life to live half American?" "Will things be better for the next generation in the peace to follow?" "Would it be demanding too much to demand full citizenship rights in exchange for the sacrificing of my life?" "Is the kind of America I know worth defending?" "Will America be a true and pure democracy after this war?" "Will Colored Americans suffer still the indignities that have been heaped upon them in the past?"[39]

The United States and its allies had adopted a V for Victory campaign. Thompson proposed in his letter that "colored Americans adopt the double VV for a double victory."[40] Black soldiers would fight fascism on the battlefield—and African Americans would fight racial discrimination in the United States. The *Courier* had fought both fights for years; therefore, it was not surprising when in the next issue (February 7),

Participants in the Double V campaign

the newspaper announced a Double V campaign. Over the next several months, the *Courier* published articles, testimonials, photographs, and drawings supporting the campaign. They received hundreds of telegrams and letters praising the campaign, and by mid-July the paper claimed that it had recruited two hundred thousand Double V members.[41]

The campaign swept the nation—well, black communities nation-wide. There were Double V dances and parades, Double V flag-raising ceremonies, Double V baseball games between black professional teams, Double V beauty contests, and a Double V song, "A Yankee Doodle Tan," introduced to a nationwide audience by NBC.[42] There was even a Double V hairstyle. The campaign was endorsed by prominent black people, including Joe Louis, Marian Anderson, Lionel Hampton, and Roy Wilkins. Fredi Washington, stage and screen actress, was one of several women listed as "Courier's 'Double V' Girl of the Week." The campaign was also endorsed by prominent whites, including Sinclair Lewis, James M. Mead, Eleanor Roosevelt, Wendell L. Willkie, more than a dozen members of Congress, and hundreds of federal and state employees.

The Double V campaign lasted a year. It did not win the war against racism in the United States—that was an unrealistic goal; however, it was impactful. Black Americans embraced the war effort. The Double V campaign also bonded black people. Double V Clubs supported the war effort by selling war bonds and collecting and sending items to black soldiers. But they also wrote letters to members of Congress to protest poll taxes, and they confronted white business leaders about their hiring practices. The campaign foreshadowed the activism that would characterize the civil rights movement.

His role with the Double V campaign did not cement Prattis's place in history; that occurred in 1947, when he was unanimously granted membership in the Senate and House press galleries by the executive committee of the Periodical Correspondents Association.[43] This recognition was heralded across Black America as a victory for the black press—and a triumph for all black Americans.

In the 1940s and 1950s, Prattis emerged as one of this country's leading journalists. Historian Charles A. Rosenberg said of Prattis, "His career, while not as widely celebrated as other newsmen, puts him on par with his generation's great journalists."[44] The historian described this period in Prattis's life:

> After World War II, he spent 10 years covering the remaking of the world, including the founding conference of the United Nations (with Rayford W. Logan, *Courier* foreign affairs editor), the reconstruction of Europe, and a series of stories on the "brown babies" born to German women by American soldiers of African descent....
> He was invited to join Dr. Ralph Bunche in Rhodes, where the United Nations diplomat was hammering together a settlement of the Arab-Israeli war that began in 1948. His 1954 series entitled "Peace Prospects in the Holy Land" drew critical acclaim from both Arab and Israeli leaders.[45]

In addition to his duties as editor, Prattis wrote a weekly column, "The Horizon," which gave him a platform for addressing racism and other topics. He wrote stories about and corresponded with many of the prominent newsmakers of his time. He interviewed or corresponded with John F. Kennedy, Haile Selassie, Eleanor Roosevelt, Malcolm X, Jackie Robinson, W.E.B. Du Bois, Richard Nixon, Franklin Delano Roosevelt, Belford Lawson, Thurgood Marshall, Elijah Muhammad, Langston Hughes, Lyndon B. Johnson, Martin Luther King Jr., and many others.

Percival Prattis (right) speaking with John F. Kennedy in 1959.

Prattis retired from the *Pittsburgh Courier* in 1965. The newspaper's circulation had precipitously dropped, and the paper was no longer profitable. The *Courier* was bought by John Sengstacke, the nephew of Prattis's old boss at the *Chicago Defender*. Prattis was seventy years old and had spent more than four decades working for newspapers—working to change the United States. It was a good time to leave.

After leaving the *Courier*, Prattis worked with civic organizations around Pittsburgh. He was the first African American officer of the Community Chest of Allegheny County, president of the Brashear Association, and vice president of the Federation of Social Agencies of Pittsburgh and Allegheny County. He sat on the boards of the Centre Avenue YMCA, the Pittsburgh branch of the NAACP, and the Urban League. He was named "Community Leader of the Year" by Jewish War Veterans Post 49. In 1962, he was awarded a medal as one of Hampton Institute's most illustrious alumni and, in 1965, was given the Master of Men award by the Pennsylvania YMCA.[46]

Prattis died February 29, 1980, at the Veterans Administration Hospital in Aspinwall, Pennsylvania. He was survived by his wife Helen Marie and his daughter Patricia. If children are our legacy, then Patricia Prattis continued the legacy of her father—and her mother, who played classical piano. In 1966, Patricia became the first black woman to be awarded a contract with a major symphony orchestra, when she was named principal keyboardist of the Pittsburgh Symphony Orchestra.

William "Bill" Gibson

Although not as heralded as Prattis, William "Bill" Gibson had a long and distinguished career as a reporter, columnist, and newspaper executive. He was one of the first black Americans to achieve fame as a sportswriter. His column, "Hear Me Talkin' to Ya," which appeared in the *Baltimore Afro-American*, cemented his popularity and influence in African American communities. It was widely read and frequently quoted. Gibson, who spent his entire career at black newspapers, was greatly respected by his colleagues. In 1946, *Color* magazine listed him among the "leading ten colored newsmen" in the country.[47]

William I. Gibson painted by Diane Cleland, 2017.

He was born in 1902, in Hampton, Virginia, to Fannie and William O. Gibson. After completing local primary and secondary schools, he attended nearby Hampton Institute from 1915 to 1920, where his father William was in charge of the general duties squad, and his mother Fannie was a teacher.[48] He enrolled at the Ferris Institute in 1922. After Ferris, he studied at Ohio State University, where he earned a bachelor's degree and a master's degree.[49]

Gibson worked briefly at the *Norfolk Journal and Guide* in Norfolk, Virginia, but his career began in earnest in 1927, when he was hired as a reporter for the *Baltimore Afro-American*. The newspaper, also known as *The Afro*, was started in 1892, by John Henry Murphy Sr., who had been enslaved. Murphy created the paper by merging his publication, *The Sunday School Helper*, with two other church publications, *The Ledger* (owned by George F. Bragg of Baltimore's St. James Episcopal Church) and the *Afro-American* (published by Reverend William M. Alexander, pastor of Baltimore's Sharon Baptist Church). By the time Gibson was hired, the newspaper had become the most widely circulated black paper along the Atlantic Coast and was an ardent foe of Jim Crow practices.[50] Its editorial page carried the slogan—"Independent in all things, neutral in nothing."

They Received AFRO-AMERICAN Staff Promotions

WILLIAM I. GIBSON   MRS. CLEMENTINE KNOX   VICTOR L. GRAY

$64,000 Paid on 'Force Mortgage

W. I. Gibson Made Editor of Afro; Others Promoted

William Gibson is shown receiving a promotion in this 1944 *Afro-American* newspaper article.

In the 1930s, the *Afro-American* was the largest black newspaper, operating its own plant, with an entirely black workforce. This was intentional. White newspapers rarely hired black employees—and those newspapers sensationalized crimes that involved black people. So Murphy dictated that the *Afro-American* hire both men and women—but only black people.

> I believe colored people can be found for any type of work we do now or ever will do. If you can't find experts, then train them yourself. How can our own people ever expect to operate complicated machinery unless they get a chance at it in our own plants?[51]

Gibson's tenure at the *Afro-American* lasted more than two decades, with him rising: sports reporter, sports editor, managing editor, and, finally, editor. His time at the newspaper, 1927 to 1952, saw the *Afro-American* intensify its fight against Jim Crow. On the local level, the newspaper crusaded for racial equality and economic advancement for African Americans in Maryland, including working to obtain equal pay for black school teachers. The paper also covered lynchings, mob actions, and peonage. The

Afro-American collaborated with the NAACP on several civil rights cases, including *Murray v. Pearson*.

All arenas in society were influenced by Jim Crow, including sports. In the South, where de jure segregation ruled, it was illegal for blacks to compete against whites. In other parts of the country, forms of de facto segregation were practiced—though not illegal, it was taboo for blacks to compete with whites. By necessity, black people

Gibson shown as managing editor of the *Afro-American*.

created their own teams, leagues, championships—and their own stars. For example, historically black colleges on the East Coast created the CIAA (originally the Colored Intercollegiate Athletic Association, now the Central Intercollegiate Athletic Association).[52] Most newspapers had little or no interest in reporting on the athletic contests between CIAA schools, but there were black Americans who were passionate about those teams, and Gibson gave them the news they wanted. One observer noted, "Gibson . . . was the first tan sportswriter of influence in the East and undoubtedly one of the most prolific journalists of the CIAA's formative years."[53]

Gibson covered local high school sports, collegiate sports (especially CIAA teams), and semi-professional and professional athletics—any sporting events involving black athletes. He reported on the Baltimore Black Sox and other teams in the Negro Leagues. In those rare instances when black athletes were allowed to compete against whites, Gibson glowingly reported on the performances of what he called the "race athletes."[54]

He also wrote a great deal about Joe Louis, perhaps the greatest heavyweight boxer in history. In 1935, Louis fought Primo Carnera, nicknamed the Ambling Alp, because he was six feet, six inches tall and weighed at least 265 pounds. The chiseled Carnera, an Italian, was a favorite of Benito Mussolini. Carnera was a strong and dangerous fighter. In 1933, he knocked out Ernie Schaaf in the thirteenth round of their bout; Schaaf died two days later. Carnera was no match for Lewis, who knocked him to the mat three times in the sixth round before the referee stopped the fight.

Gibson wrote about the fight—and Louis's performance—with a blend of admiration and hyperbole:

> Persons who saw the leather hurricane from Detroit raze the Italian Mountain to sea level, came away thoroughly convinced that Lewis is the finest piece of fighting machinery they've seen in action in over a decade. In the condition that he was Tuesday night, Joe could have taken on Baer, Braddock and Schmeling, all on the same night, and come up smiling.[55]

Two years later, Louis won the heavyweight title, a belt he successfully defended twenty-five times. He was a hero to black Americans, living proof that a black man could be the best in the world at something. Black Americans sat glued to their radios to listen to Louis's fights. When he won, they felt as if they had won. When Louis lost, they were heartbroken.

Gibson knew the challenges faced by black people in all walks of life, including athletics. He knew the unfairness of Jim Crow laws and customs in the South *and* North. Even when black athletes were allowed to play on "white teams," they faced prejudice from opponents—and teammates. He knew about the experiences of Gideon Smith, Belford Lawson, and other black pioneers of intercollegiate sports. Decades after their experiences, black athletes still faced significant challenges when they played on integrated teams.

> The colored star, as most of us know, must be extraordinarily good in order to get his chance. The truth of it is he must be THE STANDOUT on the team. He can't be just as good as some white player, he must be better than the best, if such is possible. Harry Kipke, head at the University of Michigan, where Willis Ward, despite his brilliance, was denied the captaincy of the Wolverine eleven, has been quoted as saying that when a colored candidate reports for the squad, he orders the rest of the squad to "level at him without mercy."[56]

Gibson was not as outspoken against racism as were Belford Lawson and Percival Prattis—or maybe he had a different approach. He sometimes discussed or mentioned instances of racism in his writing and matter-of-factly condemned this injustice, but his focus was on celebrating African American achievement, on and off playing fields. His reputation as a journalist was derived more from his thorough, nuanced writing about black athletes than for a sustained attack on racism. The *Afro-American* was a newspaper read by black Americans nationally, but there was only one instance where Gibson was drawn into a nationwide story about race. That incident reveals a lot about what it was like to be a black person, even one of prominence, during the Jim Crow 1940s.

In 1944, a group of black newspaper publishers met at a party in New York's Roosevelt Hotel, a week before the Republican convention. A photographer from *Life* magazine was there, presumably to take pictures of Thomas E. Dewey, the Republican candidate for president. The magazine later published two photographs.

DEWEY MEETS THE NEGRO PUBLISHERS

Dewey shakes hands with Eustace Gay, city editor of Philadelphia *Tribune*. Standing with a drink is William Gibson, managing editor of Baltimore *Afro-American*.

William Gibson listens to presidential candidate Thomas Dewey in 1944 *Life* magazine photo.

> One showed Dewey "sharing a joke" with Robert Durr of the *Birmingham Weekly*, Dr. C.B. Powell of *Amsterdam News*, New York, and John Sangstacke [*sic*] of the *Chicago Defender*. The other, *Life* said, pictured the Republican nominee smiling as he shook hands with Eustace Gay, city editor of the *Philadelphia Tribune*. Standing with them, *Life* said, was William Gibson, managing editor of the *Baltimore Afro-American*, with a drink in his hand. Neither picture showed Dewey drinking or holding a glass.[57]

Governor Olin D. Johnston of South Carolina, a candidate for the Democratic nomination for the United States Senate seat from South Carolina, saw an opportunity to appeal to the white supremacist leanings of his political base.[58] In a radio address, Johnson said:

> If additional proof is needed that South Carolinians should remain Democratic, look at the Republican nominee as he attended a Negro drinking party as pictured in the issue of *Life* magazine of July 3, 1944. President Roosevelt has never been pictured at a Negro liquor party.[59]

D. Arnett Murphy, 57, has been with the paper 40 years, is proud of fact that he has worked his way from sweeping floors to V-Pres. and Advertising Head of Co.

Heavy (212 lbs.), easy-going, cigar-chewing Cliff Mackay, come to tough Managing Editor spot on Afro from Atlanta Daily World in '45.

Tough, poker-faced Furman L. Templeton, personnel director of Afro and Carl Murphy's trouble-shooter, was with Urban League.

YOU'VE seen Baltimore through the eyes of the *Afro*. Now take a look at the people who produce the *Afro*. In its 57 years of existence the *Afro* has built itself a large, smoothly functioning staff. More than any other Negro paper, it has made a point of hiring experienced, well-trained men. Editor Bill Gibson believes that the future of Negro publications depend only on the integrity and intelligence of their personnel. The result is obvious in the *Afro's* exhaustive coverage which hit its peak during the war. Their correspondent Ollie Stewart became famous then.

The *Afro* also makes its share of mistakes. It is still plagued with an occasional libel suit which slips into its 14 editions. But the little news sheet which the late John H. Murphy bought with $200 borrowed from his wife has come of age. For one thing it has a blooming 207,324 national circulation (ABC) and the biggest advertising lineage (144,200 per week) of any Negro weekly. Two hopes of its founder still remain dear to it. It is the magic carpet of the Murphy family. And it never uses the word *Negro*. The old "chief" preferred "colored."

Howard H., one of sons of George B., is Business Mgr., an easy-going Murphy.

Bettye, fast-talking daughter of Carl Murphy, is Asst. Man. Ed., Bd. member.

Big "Bill" Gibson whom staff still calls "Boss Man" became first person outside of Murphy clan to get on Editorial Board, is now Editor of chain.

END

OUR WORLD October   PAGE 27

William Gibson and other *Afro-American* staff were featured in the May 1949 issue of *Our World* magazine.

This was an obvious attempt to brand Dewey, as a supporter of social equality, a violator of the South's racial norms. Dewey lost the election, though there is no evidence that Johnston's theatrics impacted the election.

Gibson remained at the *Afro-American* until 1952, when he became the executive editor for Johnson Publishing, the company that published *Ebony*, *Jet*, and *Tan* magazines. He also became a professor of English and journalism and director of public relations at Morgan State University. He remained in both positions until 1954, when he became director of public relations for Bennett College. In 1966, Gibson accepted a position as a copy editor for the Baltimore-based *News American*, a position he held until his retirement, in 1974.

One final note about Gibson. He married Ivora King, who was also an accomplished journalist. She was one of the first African American women to earn a living as a sportswriter. Her column, "Women in Sports," ran in the *Afro-American* in 1931 and 1932. She used her writing to offer an early black feminist perspective on sports.

Russell A. Dixon painted by Diane Cleland, 2017.

The black dentist-citizen-businessman . . . must continue
giving of his time and energies to serve as centers of
influence in guiding the destinies of his community.

—James W. Holley

Foster Kidd, *Profile of the Negro in American Dentistry* (Washington, DC: Howard University Press, 1979), 66.

Fixing More Than Teeth: African American Dentists

Ferris Institute was a vital part of the pipeline from Hampton to schools of dentistry. Students from Hampton came to Ferris to take science courses. After completing their Ferris coursework, they enrolled in the dental schools at Howard University, the University of Michigan, Northwestern University, or Marquette University.

Arthur James (A.J.) Wells received a diploma/certificate in bricklaying from Hampton in 1913. The following year, he enrolled in the college preparatory program at Ferris, remaining from 1914 to 1916. Wells earned his Doctor of Dental Surgery (DDS) degree from Northwestern University in 1919. In 1924, he was the vice president of the Old Dominion State Dental Association; he became president in 1950. Wells was listed in the 1942 edition of *Who's Who in Colored America*. Charles L. Pope was a student at Hampton in 1917. When he left Hampton, he took a job on the Canadian Pacific Railroad. After a couple of years, he enrolled at Ferris. Later, he attended Marquette Dental College in Milwaukee, and eventually practiced dentistry there. Ernest Folsom Anderson took business courses at Hampton until 1919 and enrolled at the Ferris Institute in 1920. He took predental courses at Tufts College and entered dental school at Harvard, where he received a degree in dentistry in 1927. Anderson practiced dentistry in New York until World War II, when he served as a dental technician at Fort Huachuca in Arizona. After the war, he operated a dental practice in Hampton, Virginia, until his death in 1954. It is not clear if Wells, Pope, or Anderson were active politically; however, there is evidence that most of the Hampton to Ferris students who became dentists became civic and civil rights leaders.[1]

Russell Dixon (middle right) pictured in the 1923 *Crimson and Gold* yearbook.

The Howard University College of Dentistry was founded in 1881, making it the fifth oldest dental school in the United States.[2] The college is housed in the Russell A. Dixon Building, named in honor of the man who served as dean from 1931 to 1966. Dixon is one of the students who came from Hampton to Ferris in the early 1900s. Although he is not as well-known as Belford Lawson and Percival Prattis, his impact on society was significant—in the course of his thirty-five-year tenure as dean, he was responsible for educating two generations of black dentists. In 1960, more than half of the nation's 1,681 African American dentists were graduates of the Howard University College of Dentistry. His students not only provided a much-needed service to black patients, they often became community leaders.

Russell was born in Kansas City, Missouri, on February 24, 1898. Lillie Belle Dixon, his mother, was a homemaker. His father, William James Dixon, was a Pullman porter and the inventor of the rerailer, a device that puts derailed cars back on the tracks. The elder Dixon's invention was featured in the 1942 radio series *Freedom's People: The Negro Worker*.[3] That is one of the rare instances where he is given credit for his creation—and there is no record that he gained any wealth from his invention. The family lived a working-class life.

Dixon's education began at Western University in Quindaro, Kansas, one of the Freedmen's Schools built after the Civil War. Western University has the distinction of being the earliest school for African Americans west of the Mississippi River. The school, which ceased operations in 1943, was only nominally a university. More correctly, it was a primary school for black students. Dixon spent two years at Western and was accredited to the eighth grade. His early ambition was to become a mechanical engineer. One of the teachers at Western recommended that he attend Hampton Institute.

It is not known if this was his first introduction to Hampton; however, it is likely that he was aware of Hampton's most famous alumni, Booker T. Washington. Dixon attended Hampton from 1918 to 1920. He was an exceptional student and a player on the institute's football team. Like Lawson and Prattis, he discovered that Hampton did not have the academic courses that he desired. So he followed the lead of others and came to Ferris.

Dixon arrived at Ferris in the fall of 1920.[4] He was enrolled in the college preparatory program for four years. Clifton Dummett, a dentist who wrote an account of Dixon's life, noted that Dixon impressed Woodbridge Ferris:

> Dixon harbored an interest in the health professions, and applied himself earnestly to his studies. He undertook odd jobs and engaged in serious extracurricular readings at the Institute library—all activities that impressed President Ferris. Ultimately, Russell Dixon opted for a career in dentistry. During his four years at the Institute, Russell enjoyed the friendship and encouragement of President Ferris who took a personal interest in this ambitious young man. It was the beginning of a lifelong relationship about which Russell always expressed everlasting gratitude.[5]

Dixon finished his undergraduate education at the Ferris Institute in 1924. Woodbridge encouraged him to continue his education at Northwestern University—and when Dixon agreed, Ferris used his influence to help Dixon gain admittance to the prestigious Northwestern University Dental School. He remained at the school for four years, maintaining a full student load while working full-time for the Illinois Central Railroad.

In 1929, Dixon completed his undergraduate degree in dental studies. He immediately enrolled in the graduate program, specializing in oral

Russell Dixon and Percy Fitzgerald at the Howard University College of Dentistry

pathology. His tuition was paid partly with fellowships from Northwestern and the Rosenwald Foundation.[6] Shortly after that, he was offered a teaching position at the Howard University School of Dentistry. This presented Dixon with a predicament. The invitation to join the Howard faculty was appealing; however, he wanted to receive his graduate degree. Fortunately, he had an ally in Arthur Davenport Black, the dean of the dental school at Northwestern. Black was a distinguished administrator and the son of G.V. Black, the father of modern dentistry.

Dean Black convinced Dixon that he should take the job at Howard; more importantly, he devised a schedule where Dixon could teach at Howard while remaining a student in good standing at Northwestern. He was allowed to complete courses in the summers. In 1933, Dixon received his Master of Science in Dentistry degree, making him one of the first black people to earn a graduate degree in dentistry.

When Dixon arrived at Howard, he was unaware of the political infighting that would engulf him. The dental school had recently become autonomous, with its own dean and faculty. Arnold Donowa, a Howard alumnus and a seasoned teacher of dentistry, was named dean. Soon after taking the post, he hired Dixon as an instructor in operative dentistry and tasked him to revamp the department.

Dean Donowa had a long-running feud with Mordecai Wyatt Johnson, the university's president—and the feud worsened. In 1931, Donowa, proud and defiant, quit his position and left Howard. The president appointed Dixon as the acting dean. This decision upset many of the dentistry faculty; Dixon was, after all, younger and less experienced than the other faculty. And he had little experience as an administrator. The criticism was not confined to Howard faculty. In a letter addressed to the president and trustees of Howard, L.H. Fairclough, chief of the Dental Department of Harlem Hospital, called Dixon's appointment a "colossal blunder." His letter was a scathing attack on President Johnson and Dixon:

> Even if I were not an alumnus of this Dental School, I have enough pride and hope for the future of the school and the progress of the dental profession, to feel that the appointment of Dr. Dixon threatens to add considerably to the already unfortunate position which the affairs of Howard University in general and the Dental School in particular, has been slowly but surely drifting. Is it a fact as I have been assured, that Dr. Dixon has never practiced his profession independently of a school, even for one single day? Is it a fact that his only experience and qualification is graduation from Northwestern University in 1929, his position as instructor in Operative Dentistry for two years at Howard University, and his presumably pursuing a course in some graduate school for the past summer session?[7]

He added that Howard University was at a "sad and sorry pass," because the president wanted to "man his faculty with puppets who must be willing to be subservient to his every whim and caprice."[8] This letter was published in several large black newspapers. Dixon immediately began work that would prove his critics wrong.

Within a year of accepting the deanship, Dixon instituted a program to upgrade the faculty—actively recruiting promising young dentists and sending current faculty to premiere dental colleges for postgraduate training. He also began a long process to earn full accreditation. In 1934, he instituted a training program for dental hygienists, the only one in metropolitan Washington, DC. In 1948, the dental school received full accreditation from the American Dental Association's Council on Education.

Dixon served as the dean for more than three decades, one of the longest tenures for a dean of a dental school in the nation, and Howard University's College of Dentistry earned an international reputation for excellence. He helped educate hundreds of dentists to provide high-quality oral health services to minority and underprivileged populations—and to provide these services with humility. In 1937, he wrote about the role of the black dentist:

> [The black dentist] is charged with the duty of spreading the gospel of oral health to the most remote community—not by remaining within the confines of his office, alone, nor by shouting from the housetops, but by walking shoulder to shoulder with his fellows as he enlightens and administers, with sympathy and understanding, to their physical well-being.[9]

In some states, it was illegal for white dentists to treat black patients. Even where it was not forbidden by law, there were Jim Crow customs which made the treatment of black patients taboo—in part, because the intimacy involved—touching faces, placing fingers in mouths—implied social equality. A white dentist also had to worry that their white patients might be offended if they discovered that the dental staff and facilities were shared with black people. In pre–civil rights movement America, black patients were almost wholly restricted to the relatively few practicing black dentists. In the 1930s, there was one white dentist for every 1,700 white people, but only one black dentist for every 6,707 black people. Dixon lamented the dearth of black dentists, especially in the South:

> In the entire South, there is only one Negro dentist for each 12,312 of Negro population. West Virginia, with a rate of one Negro dentist to each 5,222 of Negro population, represents the most favorable condition (though far short of a reasonable quota) to be found in the

South; with Mississippi, on the other hand, with a ratio of one Negro dentist to each 34,818 Negroes, representing the other extreme.[10]

The supporters of Jim Crow segregation used many strategies to keep black people from acquiring graduate school education in the South. In some instances, states approved scholarships that could be applied to tuition—if the black student left the state to attend a northern school. In other cases, a state might hastily construct an "institution" for black students. Dixon saw these tactics as ruses, deception by stratagem.

> There is no doubt but that the solution of the problem of supplying more Negro dentists lies in the provision of greater opportunities. The dental schools of the United States, generally, both North and South, should open their doors for the admission of well-qualified Americans regardless of race or religion. The building of any additional dental schools, exclusively for Negroes, should be tabooed on the grounds that it is undemocratic, wasteful of resources, stultifying to progress and highly embarrassing to America in perpetuating an antiquated, unchristian practice aimed to maintain suppression and mediocrity.[11]

Dixon recognized that the fight to improve the lives of black people had to be fought on multiple fronts. White supremacist policies—like all-white dental associations—should be opposed. In 1962, he was part of a team of black dentists that persuaded the American Dental Association (ADA) to strip voting powers from state and local ADA affiliates that barred blacks from membership.[12] Despite facing institutional and individual racism, black people had to "own" their destinies. For Dixon, this meant creating opportunities for young black men and women to excel as health professionals.

In 1955, the dental school moved into a newly constructed building. The state-of-the-art facility cost $3.5 million (33.5 million in 2020 dollars). It included a general clinic, four preclinical laboratories, classrooms, an extensive library, a

Russell Dixon receives keys to the new dental building at Howard University in 1955.

cafeteria, and a shared study and lounge area. The building accommodated 400 students, allowing an increase in undergraduate students from 205 to 320 undergraduates. The new facility allowed enrollment in the dental hygiene program to increase from 17 to 80 students. In 1960, *Ebony* magazine highlighted the growth of the dental school under Dixon's leadership. The faculty had grown from 15 to 50, and student enrollment had grown from 40 to 248, with students from eighteen countries.[13] The diversity of the student body reflected Dixon's commitment to racial and ethnic integration.

Recognition

Dixon was a pioneering dental professional who lived most of his life during the Jim Crow period. This meant that like Percival Prattis and Belford Lawson, Dixon was often the first (or second) black American to receive a particular recognition. In 1933, he became the first African American to earn an advanced degree in dentistry from Northwestern. In 1961, he was elected to the fellowship of the American College of Dentists, becoming the second African American so honored. In 1963, President Kennedy appointed him a regent of the National Library of Medicine, the first time a black person held that position. He was appointed to the board of directors of the National Health Council in 1967. In 1968, He received the William J. Gies Award, the highest award given by the American College of Dentists.

Dixon served as president of the Pan-American Odontological Association. He was an honorary lifetime member of the Robert T. Freeman Dental Society—an organization named in honor of the first professionally trained black dentist in the United States.[14] He was also a contributing member of the National Association on Standard Medical Vocabulary, the Odonto-Chirurgical Society of Philadelphia, and the Maimonides Society of the District of Columbia. Like many of the Hampton/Ferris men, he was deeply religious, which partly explains his participation on the race relations committee of the United Church of Christ.[15]

In 1955, Northwestern University honored Dixon's contributions by granting him the Alumni Award of Merit and, in 1964, by conferring upon him an honorary doctorate.[16] The next year, he received an honorary doctorate from Ferris State College. But, the biggest honor came posthumously. In 1981, Howard University placed his name on the College of Dentistry building.

Percy A. Fitzgerald

Percy A. Fitzgerald distinguished himself as the head of the Prosthodontia Department of Howard University—after serving in the famed Harlem Hellfighters regiment during World War I. In his youth, he was celebrated as a hero; later, he was hailed as a wise and compassionate teacher. He was born to Alex and Eva Fitzgerald on April 19, 1896, in Blackstone, Virginia, one of eight children born to the couple. Fitzgerald was graduated from the Hampton Institute in 1917. He taught briefly in Blackstone before joining the Army on October 27, 1917. Fitzgerald was sent to France during World War I; while there he was transferred to the 15th New York Colored Infantry Regiment as supply sergeant. The 15th Infantry was later renamed the 369th Infantry.

Percy A. Fitzgerald painted by Diane Cleland, 2017.

In the early 1900s, it was common to hear whites—including military officers—claim that blacks were unfit to serve in combat units. Black men, it was argued, lacked the intelligence, discipline, and courage to succeed on the battlefield. Today, it is easy to see that these beliefs reflected racial prejudice and served as a justification for discrimination against the black people who served in the American military during World War I.

The 369th Infantry was an African American unit. Most people know it by a nickname, the Harlem Hellfighters. It was one of the few black combat regiments. Its members' training took place in Spartanburg, South Carolina—but training was interrupted, because southern military officials "refused to have their men exposed to northern niggers."[17] When they arrived in Europe for duty, they were segregated from white soldiers—and, adding insult, they spent months as stevedores. On April 8, 1918, the United States Army assigned the unit to the French Army, in large part because many white American soldiers refused to perform combat duty with black soldiers. The French unit had been depleted, so they welcomed the black soldiers, who they called the Men of Bronze.

The Germans who fought the men from the 369th had a different name for the unit: the Hellfighters. This was a compliment, a term of respect. The Hellfighters served 191 days under fire. That represents more time in continuous combat than any other American unit. Undermining the racist contention that black men were Toms and Sambos who lacked courage, they fought and won many battles, despite suffering the most losses of any American regiment, with 1,500 casualties. In a letter written while in France, Fitzgerald described one of the unit's battles:

> During the big drive which started on the night of September 25 our boys took an active part. The regiment was in for twelve days and came out much smaller than it went in. Most of the fighting was in the open with no trenches.[18]

The Hellfighters claim to have never lost a man through capture, lost a trench, or lost a foot of ground to the enemy. Those bold claims are difficult to prove. There is, however, no dispute that the French soldiers saw the Hellfighters as courageous fighters. The French army bestowed on the Hellfighters the prestigious Croix de Guerre for "brave and bitter fighting."[19]

They returned to a parade in Harlem (their original home), greeted by at least a million supporters. But when the parade ended, they were still confronted by Jim Crow racism in the South and racial segregation in the North—worse still, they returned to a country that was soon to be gripped by the race riots of 1919.

After the war, Fitzgerald enrolled at the Ferris Institute. He was graduated from the college preparatory program in 1920 and went on to study dentistry at Northwestern University. In 1924, Fitzgerald earned his DDS from Northwestern University and practiced dentistry in the Chicago area until 1931.[20] At that time, he joined the teaching faculty of Howard University. Realizing the necessity of continued study, Fitzgerald

Negro D. D. S. Gets High Degree

Dr. Percy A. Fitzgerald, who in 1931 was appointed a member of the dental staff at Howard University, has just been awarded the degree of M. S. D. (Master of Science in Dentistry) by Northwestern University. This is the second M. S. D. degree to be awarded by Northwestern to a Negro, the first having been given to Dr. Russell A. Dixon, dean of the College of Dentistry at Howard. Dr. Fitzgerald is an alumnus of Northwestern, having received the degree D. D. S. in 1924.

Percy Fitzgerald received many honors.

began postgraduate work in ceramics at Northwestern University Dental School in the summer of 1933.[21] In 1936, he became the second African American to earn a Master's of Science in Dentistry from Northwestern, being preceded by Russell A. Dixon, his colleague and the dean at Howard University. In 1936, Fitzgerald was named the head of the Prosthodontia Department at Howard.

Fitzgerald had a distinguished career as a practicing professional, researcher, and teacher. He was a professor of dentistry at Howard University for over thirty years and was named national Dentist of the Year in 1959. He was a charter member of Omicron Kappa Upsilon, a national honor society for dentistry, a member of the National Dental Association, and a visiting lecturer at Meharry Medical College in Nashville, Tennessee. Today, Howard University dental students compete for the Percy A. Fitzgerald Outstanding Achievement Award in clinical crown and bridge.

Community and Civic Leaders

From the 1930s through the 1960s, it was common for dentists to take active roles in—indeed, often to lead—the civil rights organizations in their communities. They were well-educated professionals whose businesses, once established, were not dependent on financial support from white people—and, therefore, could not be threatened with the withdrawal of that support. Lawrence E. (L.E.) Paxton, who attended Hampton from 1915 to 1917, before coming to Ferris, is an example.[22] In 1959, Paxton served as the president of the Citizens' Protective Association, a group in Roanoke, Virginia, that advocated for the fair treatment of African Americans by banks, lenders, and other community organizations. He was a member of the Roanoke School Board in 1964, the only black member of the school board at the time.

Nathaniel P. Miller's life and activism are also instructive. He was graduated from Hampton in 1914. In a farewell address to his fellow students, Miller offered an optimistic, though inexperienced, assessment of race relations:

> The time has passed, when a man is recognized and given a high seat by society because of his rank and ancestry. He is now honored for his ability. The world is waiting with outstretched arms, ready to receive the man, regardless of race, rank, creed or color, who can and does produce the goods. It is willing to give him a fair trial. It is

saying "Let the best man win, whoever he is." The age demands men whose feet stand on the ground, who can see things as they really are, and act accordingly."[23]

He was, unfortunately, wrong. The United States in 1914 was more than a generation away from removing Jim Crow laws—and much farther away from eliminating the importance of race as a determinate of one's life chances. To his credit, Miller spent much of his life combating racial injustice. After completing the college preparatory program at Ferris, he studied at the Northwestern University Dental School. After he was graduated in 1929, he returned to the South, practicing dentistry in Farmville, Virginia, for over fifty years. He served as president of the local National Association for the Advancement of Colored People (NAACP), trying to create a society "ready to receive the man, regardless of race, rank, creed or color."

In 1959, officials in Prince George County refused to levy taxes to operate schools. This was their response to court orders to desegregate. Without the necessary tax revenue, all schools in the county were closed. The shutdown lasted for five years. During this time, Miller's dental office served as a classroom for students, and it served as a meeting place for civil rights groups and protesters. In 1969, five years after the public schools reopened, Miller was named to the school board, making him the first African American to serve in that capacity.

The Sad Story of Maceo Alston Santa Cruz

Black people who violated Jim Crow norms risked their bodies and their lives. African American dentists—with greater education, wealth, and autonomy than other black people—were more likely to challenge the existing racial norms. And when they ignored society's racial script, they were severely punished. In 1921, Lafayette Cockrell, a black dentist, pled guilty to "associating with" a white woman. He was fined a thousand dollars, the limit under the law. This punishment did not please local whites. A white mob abducted Cockrell. He was found in a deserted farmhouse. Newspapers reported that he had been "operated upon" and that his injury was "permanent."[24] In 1924, H. Brummitt, president of the Alabama Negro Medical Dental and Pharmaceutical Association, was forcibly removed from his home and flogged by angry whites. Members of the mob told him he was whipped because he practiced dentistry on white patients. He was also ordered to leave town within ninety days.[25] In 1925,

R. Ward, a black dentist in Houston, was "called from his home, seized by three men disguised as negroes, and taken to the outskirts of Houston in an automobile."[26] His attackers removed his clothing, painted him with tar, applied feathers, and poured acid on his hands. They also robbed him of his money and watch. No reason was given for the torture. Unfortunately, attacks on African Americans, including black dentists, did not end in the 1920s. The case of Maceo Alston Santa Cruz is instructive.

Maceo Alston Santa Cruz pictured with other college preparatory students in 1919–1920 class.

Santa Cruz was born on July 20, 1898. He attended Hampton until 1919, and he was enrolled at Ferris Institute from 1921 to 1923. Like several of his African American colleagues at Ferris in the 1920s, he became a dental student at Howard University, graduating in 1927. The following year, Santa Cruz went to Pulaski, Virginia, and established himself as that city's first African American dentist. He married Cathleen Jenkins, a local teacher, and became an active civic leader—a member of the American Legion, the Knights of Pythias, the Magic City Medical Society, and the NAACP. As much as was possible for an African American living in the Jim Crow South, Santa Cruz was living the American Dream.

That dream ended on February 6, 1951.

Shortly after leaving his office, Santa Cruz happened upon an altercation between two young white men and two African American girls, Evelyn Bland, seventeen, and Marie French, fourteen. The two men were E. Buford Owen, eighteen, and Charlie Simmons, twenty. Some newspapers reported that the men were "molesting" the girls.[27] Although the details are not clear, it is likely that the girls were the victims of catcalls and groping or attempts to grope. Santa Cruz saw Simmons push French, the younger girl, against a building. He also saw Owen punch Bland in the right eye. He told the men to leave the girls alone. This plea (or order) angered Owen, who tried unsuccessfully to punch the dentist. Santa Cruz crossed the street to call the police from an emergency telephone. One of the men said, "Let's get him."

Sentenced for Molesting Teen-Age Girls, Face Murder Charge

Santa Cruz Slayers Guilty of Attacks

PULASKI, Va.—The two white men charged with the murder last week of Dr. M. A. Santa Cruz waived preliminary hearings here Friday and their cases were sent on to the Pulaski County Grand Jury.

However, the men, Charles Simmons, 20, and E. Buford Owen, 18, were found guilty, fined $100 each and sentenced to twelve months in jail on charges of assaulting the teen-age girls whom Dr. Santa Cruz gave his life to protect.

Simmons pleaded innocent and Owen pleaded guilty to the as—

(Continued on Page 4, Col. 1)

DR. M. A. SANTA CRUZ
. . . died protecting girls

E. BUFORD OWEN
. . . held for murder

CHARLIE SIMMONS
. . . helped kill dentist

The killing of Maceo Alston Santa Cruz received national attention, especially in black newspapers.

The two men attacked Santa Cruz from behind. They pulled him away from the phone. Owen held the dentist by his coat lapel while Simmons struck him. Santa Cruz fell to the concrete pavement, striking his head. He was rushed to a Roanoke hospital but was pronounced dead on arrival. Charles M. Irvin, Roanoke coroner, said that Santa Cruz died of a fractured skull and a brain hemorrhage. Owen and Simmons were charged with murder. Hubert Matthews Costigan, a taxi driver, was charged with "aiding and abetting," because he carried them away from the scene. Mayor Howard R. Imboden made the following statement:

> The fatal attack on Dr. M.A. Santa Cruz on Main St. last night was an unprovoked act and is deeply lamented by all the people of Pulaski. Dr. Santa Cruz was one of our community leaders, highly respected by both our Negro and white residents, a man who was keenly interested in our civic life and a Christian gentlemen. . . . Pulaski will miss Dr. Santa Cruz. We offer our deepest sympathy to his family and loved ones.[28]

The mayor then praised the local citizens—presumably the African Americans—for not rioting. He said, "I am proud of the fact that our citizens acted calmly in a situation which might have stirred up a serious aftermath."[29] The citizens did not riot; instead, an interracial group started a fund to engage special counsel to assist the state in prosecuting the men who killed the highly respected dentist.[30]

At trial, the two men admitted that they had been drinking alcohol before the murder, and they admitted attacking the girls; however, Simmons claimed that he struck Santa Cruz "after the doctor motioned to some Negroes standing on a nearby corner."[31] On June 30, 1951, an all-white jury found Simmons and Owen guilty of involuntary manslaughter. The jury of eleven men and one woman recommended that the two assailants be given five-year penitentiary sentences.

Untitled mural in downtown Big Rapids, Michigan.

History is the memory of mankind. It promotes heroes.
It depicts heritage. It develops pride. It promotes
dignity. To be without a history is to be a non-person.

—Robert M. Coatie

"Munsonians Celebrate Black History Month," *Muncie Evening Press*, February 16, 1980, 3.

Last Words

by Franklin Hughes

A mural troubles me.

It is a fabulous work of art. I am not an artist, but I can appreciate the vibrant and bold colors, the striking images, and the meticulous design. A mural, as public art, should say something meaningful to people for years to come. This one does that, and that is what bothers me.

I see it when I go downtown. Each time. It would be hard not to see it. The painting is large, 12' × 64', consisting of two dozen 4' × 8' panels, and it is located on the north side of the Fairman Building at one of the few busy intersections in the small town.[1] The mural is prominently displayed, so I see it, and so does anyone else passing through Big Rapids, in Mecosta County, Michigan.

I am troubled, because this beautiful piece of art tells an incomplete—and, therefore, flawed—story. The artist was charged with capturing a slice of the area's history, more specifically, its origins as a bustling center of logging. The painting does not depict a single person of color, even though black people and people with multiracial backgrounds were significant in the history of Mecosta County and neighboring Isabella, Montcalm, and Chippewa Counties. It is hard to imagine any longtime resident of this area not knowing about groups like the Old Settlers, who settled in these Michigan counties as early as the 1860s. According to a historical marker at one of the Old Settler sites in Mecosta County:

> In the 1860s Negroes from southern Michigan, Ohio and southwest Ontario settled this region as farmers and woodsmen. Some of them moved to new villages in Mecosta and Isabella counties. Schools

African American loggers were active in Mecosta County in late 1800s and early 1900s. Bessie Green Jackson is shown holding the reins.

and churches founded in the area were integrated. Among these was the Wheatland Church of Christ, established in nearby Remus in 1869. Their pioneering spirit provided unity that has led to the Old Settlers' reunions that occur annually at this spot, the homestead of one of the early families. The picnics date back to the 1890s.[2]

The artist, John Kuna, is a Canadian citizen born in Czechoslovakia. He studied at Ontario College of Art and Design and began specializing in murals soon after graduation. Kuna was commissioned by the Festival of the Arts, the Big Rapids Housing Commission, and the City of Big Rapids to create the mural. He came to Big Rapids to view the Fairman Building, meet with residents and committee members, examine various photographs, and start imagining a vision of the project. The mural was unveiled in 2018.

I wish he had met with me and my wife, Jacklyn Hughes. Of course, we would have told him about the Old Settlers—Jacklyn is a direct descendant. We would have shown him pictures of African American loggers who lived, worked, and died in this area—pictures of the Bundy Hills lumber camps, the Skinner camp, and many other pictures of African American loggers on the Muskegon River. We would have given him a more accurate story about the early days of this area.

The Thomas Cross family was one of the early black families in Mecosta County. The patriarch of the family (in the middle) was the great-great-grandfather of Jacklyn Hughes, wife of one of the authors of this book.

The 1900 U.S. Census revealed that Mecosta County had many farms owned by African Americans—the only Michigan counties with more were Cass, Isabella, and Van Buren. The mural purports to portray logging in this area for that year. Is it possible that the artist did not locate early images of African American loggers? A little research would have led him—and the local historical societies—to a *Michigan History* magazine article, published in 1987, which explored Mecosta County. It included images of local African Americans, including loggers.[3]

Even a cursory review of local history reveals a strong African American presence in the early days of Big Rapids and the surrounding areas. In addition to Old Settler communities in Mecosta, Isabella, and Montcalm Counties, nearby places like Idlewild, Baldwin, and Woodland Park have rich multicultural histories. Many famous and influential African Americans—Charles Chestnut, W.E.B. Du Bois, Joe Louis, Madam C.J. Walker, and Louis Armstrong, to name but a few—made their way to Idlewild and Baldwin from the early 1900s through the mid-1960s.[4]

I am not troubled because the mural lacks "diversity"; that is too simplistic. I am troubled because it is not historically accurate. This beautiful

The descendants of the Old Settlers gather annually at School Section Lake, a county park in Mecosta County.

mural, well-placed downtown, will, for many years, perpetuate a narrative that ignores the contributions—even the existence—of the African Americans who helped build this area. I am troubled because time and time again the contributions of peoples of color are either forgotten or considered unimportant.

When David Pilgrim asked me to find an image of Gideon Smith, so that he could commission a sculpture or painting, it set me on a journey to find truths from the past, whether they were in history books, murals, or neither. I was relatively new to this type of research. I had been an employee at Ferris since the fall of 2011. Most of my work involved digital media projects for the Diversity and Inclusion Office and the Jim Crow Museum. I had done some research for the Museum, but I assumed that all the important stories about Ferris—the man and the university—were already known. I figured there might be a couple of images in the yearbooks that we could use for reference points. That would be it. But what I found drove me to look for more. The more I learned, the more I wanted to learn.

I cross-referenced the photographs with data from the *Southern Workman* digital archives, and one thing became clear: many of the young African Americans who attended Ferris Institute from 1910 to the mid-1920s were from Virginia. During this period, there were more African American men at Ferris from Virginia than from Michigan. I knew Gideon Smith had attended Hampton Institute, but now I had a new question, "Why did other young men from Hampton come to Ferris?" The pursuit of a definitive answer—one that continues to be elusive—led to hours examining early Ferris publications, especially yearbooks. This research provided small snapshots into a different time and introduced me to stories that were long ago lost.

David Pilgrim shared my excitement. He had hoped to find a way to celebrate a single African American, Gideon Smith, but my research revealed that there were several—most notably, Belford Lawson, Percival Prattis, and Russell Dixon—who made significant societal contributions. I was excited to take information back to Pilgrim. He shared my belief that this was an important story. We then began researching as a team, compiling our respective findings. He then shared our early results with David Eisler, president of Ferris State University, who encouraged us to present our preliminary findings/discoveries to the university.

Maceo Clarke (top right) is pictured with the 1920–1921 noncommissioned officers of the Ferris Institute ROTC.

Some of what we discovered was disappointing.

We found a 1914 Ferris Institute calendar. A picture of campus life accompanies each month. Above November is a picture of students who acted in the play *Mock Trial*. Most of the three dozen students are fashionably dressed, except those who play the role of criminals. They wear raggedy clothes—and blackface makeup.[5] Not coincidently, at the time of the play the nation's newspapers routinely carried sensationalized stories about Negro criminals. The play perpetuated the narrative that black criminality was natural and inevitable—controlled, judged, and punished by whites.

That was not the only time that whites darkened their skin—pretending to be black people—to entertain audiences at Ferris Institute. In 1917, local amateur actors performed Walter Ben Hare's comedic play

This picture of a Bible class taught by Gerrit Masselink (front row, center) in 1922 shows African American students fully integrated with other students.

Much Ado about Betty on campus. The play includes two black characters, Pearlie Brown, a black maid, and Archie, a black bellboy. Pearlie's character was adorned in dark make-up; Archie was played with burnt cork or black grease paint. A basic premise of these and similar portrayals is that "Negroes—even fake ones—are funny."[6]

Hare's play was a nationwide success, typically performed as the senior class production in high schools and colleges and as a fundraiser for community groups. Wherever it was performed, newspaper reviews lauded it as a clever and funny play. Nowhere did we find criticism— voices acknowledging that blackface performances were demeaning to black people. Surely, this was a product of the times. In the early 1900s, amateur minstrel shows were considered harmless fun.

I was bothered by the blackface performers on Ferris Institute stages, but I was more troubled by something said by Gerrit Masselink, an early instructor at the institute.[7] During a lecture at a teachers' conference, he gave "an illustration of negro boys at both the Ferris Institute and the M.A.C., who have worked their way through these institutes against the most bitter prejudice, and are winning every day in their various lines of vocations."[8]

What is meant by "most bitter prejudice?"

Was Masselink alluding to the Ku Klux Klan in Mecosta County? In the 1920s, there was a significant Klan presence in Michigan—membership estimates range from 70,000 to 265,000—and there were several hundred Klan members in Mecosta County.[9] This was rural, small-town America, and Klan membership represented a defensive reaction to large-scale immigration. America, they feared, would be less white and less Protestant. The Klansmen in this county—and they were mostly men—mouthed the usual white supremacy talk, but their everyday focus was area Catholics. There is no evidence that the Klan or its sympathizers ever got a foothold at Ferris Institute.

Masselink was not the typical Ferris employee. He began as an instructor, teaching mathematics, science, and Bible study. Following Woodbridge Ferris's election as governor in 1912, Masselink regularly acted as the head of Ferris Institute. As such, he held a variety of titles from acting president to manager and vice president. And when Woodbridge died in 1928, Masselink became the second president of Ferris Institute. He shared Woodbridge's commitment to educating all students, regardless of race, sex, nationality, or class background. By all accounts, Masselink was a kind and empathetic figure, deeply involved in the everyday lives of the students. For several years, he wrote letters to the registrar at Hampton praising the work ethic of the men who came to Ferris from Hampton. He was aware when black students could not find housing, were the victims of slurs, or were otherwise mistreated because of their race/skin color. Prejudice against those students—or any students—bothered him.

I was heartened that Masselink added that the black students, despite facing prejudice, were "winning every day in their various lines of vocations." These were the years when Jim Crow practices ruled the nation, South and North. Yes, they faced racial prejudices, but African Americans had real opportunities at Ferris Institute. This section of Michigan was a space where people of color found employment, owned property, earned quality educations, sent their children to integrated schools, and enjoyed their lives in relative peace. It is not insignificant that leaders pooled monies to support a "colored" baseball team in 1902, and hundreds of people came out and cheered Booker T. Washington when he came here. I believe it says something positive that a prominent African American, John Bush, sent his son Chester to the Ferris Institute in 1903.

From this project, I gained a greater appreciation for the pursuit of truth—and for the certain truths revealed, most notably, that Ferris Institute, under the leadership of Woodbridge Ferris, was an environment—though hardly perfect—where African Americans could be successful.

Lieutenant Leonard McLeod and Military Men

On April 2, 1917, President Woodrow Wilson spoke before a special session of Congress to ask for a formal declaration of war. He proposed that the participation of the United States in the war would make the world "safe for democracy." Four days later, Congress passed the war resolution that brought the United States into World War I.

Blacks were more likely than whites to be drafted and to be placed in labor battalions. Roughly four hundred thousand African Americans served in the war effort, accounting for 13 percent of the armed services; 92 percent were

Lieutenant Leonard L. McLeod is pictured in a 1917 Hampton class picture. Image used courtesy of Hampton University Archives.

draftees, a much higher rate than of whites.[10] These men served in segregated units controlled by white officers. Most, like Percival Prattis, were assigned to complete menial nonmilitary tasks, such as working on kitchen and cleaning details. Others, including Percy Fitzgerald, engaged in intense combat.

Almost all of the students who came from Hampton to Ferris served in the war effort, either stateside or overseas. Some like Jasper C. Godwin from Smithfield, Virginia—graduated from the Hampton Institute in 1918, was active in the military, then enrolled at Ferris Institute—served without distinction. Others, including Leonard L. McLeod, were historically significant.

McLeod was born on February 17, 1893, in Key West, Florida, and attended the Hampton Institute as a student from 1915 until 1917. That year, he was selected to attend the Training Camp for Negro Officers at Fort Des Moines, Iowa, the first United States program to train and commission African American soldiers.[11] This program was a result of the advocacy of Joel Spingarn, a board member of the National Association for the Advancement of Colored People (NAACP), and like-minded people, who demanded that African American soldiers receive training to become officers. This segregated camp was needed because the army refused to integrate its officer training facilities.

The 17th Provisional Training Regiment was made up of 1,250 black candidates.[12] A thousand students and faculty were recruited from the country's best universities and colleges—Ivy League schools, Howard University, Amherst College, the Hampton and Tuskegee Institutes, and others—joined by 250 noncommissioned officers from the 9th and 10th Cavalry "Buffalo Soldiers" and the 24th and 25th Infantry. After completing the four months of rigorous and technical training, 639 graduated as newly commissioned captains and lieutenants. Some received additional preparation before being sent to units in France during World War I; while others, like McLeod, were sent to colleges to head Reserve Officers' Training Corps (ROTC) units. The success of training units at Fort Des Moines helped to undermine the prevailing belief that African Americans lacked the mental abilities and courage to be successful as soldiers—and military leaders. Their success helped lay the groundwork that resulted in President Harry Truman's executive order issued in July 1948 that abolished racial discrimination and ended segregation in the U.S. Armed Forces.

In December 1918, Secretary of War Newton D. Baker authorized colleges to establish ROTC. Hampton Institute established an ROTC, with McLeod, then a lieutenant, designated as the military instructor. Although McLeod did not serve overseas, his training of young men in military science and tactics had value. In 1919, he was given the responsibility of commanding fifty cadets, whites and blacks, at Camp Devens in Massachusetts. This was a rare opportunity for a black man.

> [Lieutenant McLeod] taught cadets from Yale, Harvard, Kemper Military Academy and the University of Alabama. The southern cadets were adamantly opposed to instruction by African American cadre and openly displayed disdain, but after two weeks the company rapport and sentiment within the company was generally good and there was no trouble.[13]

In 1920, the War Department reorganized ROTC programs, resulting in Lieutenant McLeod losing his position as an instructor, even though inspectors of the program were "impressed with the condition and performance of the ROTC battalion" under his command.[14] According to the

At least twelve African American students, including Belford Lawson, Maceo Alston Santa Cruz, Jasper Godwin, Maceo Clarke, Hannibal Clarke, L.M. Miles, and Charles Jackson, appear in this photograph of Ferris ROTC platoons 1 and 2.

Southern Workman, the Hampton ROTC was not a military instruction institution, because Hampton's charter was not "essentially military." The unit was redesignated a junior unit. Lieutenant McLeod's commission was reclassified to that of an emergency officer—in part, due to a failed physical—and he was relieved of his duties at the Hampton ROTC and replaced by Lieutenant Colonel Clifton R. Norton.[15] McLeod decided to attend the Ferris Institute to further his studies and, like many others, he enrolled in the College Preparatory Department.[16]

It is noteworthy that while McLeod was here, Ferris had racially integrated ROTC units. In a 1920 Ferris advertisement, there is a picture of the second platoon, which shows thirty-three students—seven are identifiably African Americans. That same year, the yearbook includes a picture of ROTC first and second platoons. There are at least twelve African Americans pictured, including Belford Lawson, Maceo Clarke, Maceo Alston Santa Cruz, Jasper Godwin, Charles Jackson, and Hannibal Clarke.[17] McLeod may also be pictured.[18] There is a significant message in the images of ROTC units. The soldiers, African Americans and whites, stand or sit next to each other. Almost all World War I units were racially segregated, and African American soldiers were disrespected in ways big and small by white soldiers. But pictures of the ROTC units at Ferris Institute show the soldiers as equals.

My research led me to the 325th Field Signal Battalion, the "first all-black Signal unit in the Army, and the only black Signal unit during World War I."[19] The 325th was a part of the all black 92nd Division. They established and repaired communication lines from the field to mission headquarters. Along with telegraphy, the signal unit members utilized pyrotechnics, signal flags, buzzers, and projector lamps for various communications. This group of soldiers had dangerous duties in a war zone.

> When the Infantry left their trenches and went "over the top" on their numerous plunges into "no mans" land, many times Signalmen went over with them, stringing out their communication wire behind them. When the big divisions rolled forward through and beyond "no mans" land, and ploughed into the belly of the enemy, Signalmen were at their sides, and at times, out in advance of the Infantry extending their communications.[20]

These men, like the Harlem Hellfighters, earned a reputation as a fearsome fighting force and the respect of the enemy and the French Units. They proved themselves capable as soldiers and communicators. I found several of these men had attended both Hampton and Ferris, including Edward P. Bouldin, who studied at Ferris after the war, before attending dental school.

Bouldin was born in Jeffers, Virginia, in 1895. He went to the Hampton Institute from 1912 to 1917. He enlisted in the Army and received his training at Camp Sherman, Ohio. From there Bouldin was sent to France and served as a Corporal in the 325th Field Signal Battalion. After the war, he attended the Ferris Institute, enrolling in the college preparatory program in 1920. Bouldin next attended the dental school at Northwestern University—following the lead of A.J. Wells and helping to lay the path for Russell Dixon and Percy Fitzgerald.[21] Thomas Purcell Lipscomb served in Company B of the 317th Engineer Battalion, part of the 92nd Division.[22] William Garrett Hearn, from Charlottesville, Virginia, served in the 325th Field Service Signal Battalion of the 92nd Division.[23]

Helping Others Rise

In 1890, Woodbridge Ferris began delivering his "Making the World Better" lecture. For the next three decades, he traveled the country delivering this talk against selfishness—a talk that challenged others, including his students, to help others rise. Even after he was long dead, graduates of Ferris Institute (now Ferris State University) were challenged to go out and make the world better. This message of serving the public good resonated with the students who came to Ferris from Hampton. One of those students, Paul Maurice Floyd, wrote these words:

> One who has caught the spirit of service at Hampton should never fail to be impressed and inspired by attending Ferris Institute. Mr. Ferris's radiant personality has in an equal measure the same effect of inspiring us to serve humanity as Dr. Gregg inspires Hampton students to live a life of service. To quote Mr. Ferris—Some people look forward to attending college with the idea that college is a place where they can secure the means of living a life of ease. They should have the aim of helping humanity to live better regardless of dollars and cents to be had for compensation.[24]

Some of the Hampton-to-Ferris students saw teaching as a way to make the world better. Walter Norfleet Lowe taught tailoring at the Robert Hungerford School in Eatonville, Florida.[25] He worked "for some time" as a tailoring instructor at the Agricultural and Mechanical Institute in Normal, Alabama (now Alabama A&M), before moving to Cincinnati, Ohio, to work for the McCall Industrial School.[26] McCall taught African American students trades—woodworking, furniture making, shoe repair, and more. Lowe served as superintendent of the school in the 1940s, and he stayed there in some capacity until the 1960s.[27] Paul J. Singleton, who graduated from the Hampton Institute in 1916, spent two years at the Ferris Institute, one year at the State Normal School in Ypsilanti (now Eastern Michigan University), and became a biology teacher at Virginia State University. Later Singleton became the principle of the Dinwiddie County Training School in McKenney, Virginia, which was the county's first black public high school.[28]

Some did it by spending their lives working in organizations geared toward helping others. Leo A. Roy was the first secretary and accountant of the Phelps Stokes Fund, a philanthropy enterprise with the original aim to improve housing for the poor in New York and aid the "education of Negroes, both in Africa and the United States, North American Indians, and needy and deserving white students."[29] The Phelps Stokes Fund modeled the practical education model of the Hampton Institute and the Tuskegee Institute and brought those principles to Africa. The fund produced two commissions on education in Africa. Those commissioned were tasked with learning about African cultures and developing educational programs for Africans similar to many practical education systems in the United States. Roy worked with the Phelps Stokes fund for thirty years before retiring in 1948.[30]

Mack D. Barlow from Roanoke, Virginia, attended the Ferris Institute from 1923 to 1925.[31] He and his father, Mack Barlow Sr., were the owners and operators of the Dumas Hotel in Roanoke, a popular destination for black people traveling during the Jim Crow period. The hotel was a featured stop in *The Negro Motorist Green Book*.[32] It was a twenty-six-room hotel complete with "the Jack and Jill Snack Bar, a dining room, barbershop, pool room, ice cream parlor, cleaning and pressing shop, and a second-floor ballroom."[33] The Dumas Hotel was the place to be for great food and to meet famous entertainers of that day, including Duke Ellington and Dizzy Gillespie. And, lest we forget, it was a place where black people could stay at a time when they were denied accommodations at white hotels.

Early African American Women at the Ferris Institute

Ellen and Richard Moore were enslaved in Kentucky. The couple had five children: Martha, Simon, Harrison, Lavina, and George. Before the Civil War, Richard escaped via the Underground Railroad, leaving behind Ellen and their children. Two of the children were sold to nearby enslavers. After the war, Ellen found her children and took them to Pennsylvania, where she rejoined her husband. In 1879, the family moved to Remus, Michigan. It was there that Harrison Moore had a daughter, Mary Ellen Moore. I mention her because she is listed in the 1913 Ferris Institute Catalog, studying Instrumental Music. After attending the Ferris Institute, Mary became a music teacher in the Wheatland, Michigan, community until her death in 1936. The Moore family is one of the early Old Settlers families in northern Michigan.

Today, more than five hundred African American women are enrolled at Ferris State University. Hazel Bass appeared in a Ferris Institute class picture in 1923.[34] Our efforts to locate African American women who predate her yielded only a few results; in part, because it is difficult to discern racial identity based on images alone—and none of the women with racially ambiguous appearances were from Virginia. I will not say that there were no African American women among the students who came from Hampton to Ferris, but we did not find a single one. This is not unexpected. The racial and gender norms of the early 1900s made it unlikely that young African American women would travel alone from Virginia to Michigan to gain a higher education. We did find a few African American female students in those early years of Ferris Institute.

In 1914, Woodbridge Ferris delivered a lecture in Mount Pleasant, Michigan. A symbolic act evidenced Ferris's popularity with the audience: they greeted him with a "handkerchief salute." Ferris used his talk as an opportunity to encourage college students in the audience—and to promote the Ferris Institute. He said:

Hazel Bass (second row, far left) in a 1923 Ferris class photo

> The only qualification a person needs to have to enter Ferris Institute is a deep down desire to learn. We take the student at the point where he is and help him to get where he wants to be. Regardless of sex, race, age, or financial condition, if a person really desires to learn, he or she will be welcome at Ferris Institute.[35]

Edith Wolter, a young white teacher, was in the audience. In a 1958 magazine article, she recounted how Woodbridge Ferris's words inspired her to help M.E. (Lizzie) Fields become a student—one of the first African American female students—at Ferris Institute. In the summer of 1915, Wolter and other teachers worked as waitresses at a summer resort at Harbor Springs. It was there that she met Fields, a forty-year-old cook. According to Wolter:

> One day I happened to find her reading in her cookbook, but the book was upside down. Jokingly, I asked if she had "upside down vision." She burst out crying and sobbed, "Honey, if I only knew how to read! I never wanted anyone to know about it, but now that

you know would you be willing to come in my room evenings and read to me?"[36]

Wolter did more than read to her, she wrote a letter to Woodbridge Ferris asking that he admit Fields to Ferris Institute. He wrote back saying that the institute did not have any "colored women," housing was a problem, and her age might be against her—but if she wanted to enter Ferris Institute, he would make sure she had a teacher. The following summer, Fields, accompanied by Wolter, arrived in Big Rapids. Woodbridge was not there, so she was greeted by Masselink, who was acting as head of the institute. According to Wolter:

> He was so nice to Lizzie! He made her feel so welcome. He had found a place for her to live where she could have kitchen privileges. When we left him, Lizzie had a good old-fashioned cry. They were tears of pure joy! We went to her rooming house and her landlady made her feel very much at home.[37]

Fields is listed in two Ferris Institute catalogs. In 1917, she is registered in the Normal Department; in 1920, she was a student in the English Department.[38] She was one of the first African American woman to attend Ferris. There was the unnamed "colored" student that we discussed at the beginning of chapter 2 and Mary Ellen Moore who predate her.

Blanche Elizabeth Coggan, née Brown, was not an African American, but she has relevance to the Ferris Institute and African American history. She was born on April 22, 1895, in Ellicott, Colorado. Her family moved to Alcona County, Michigan, in 1902. From 1911 to 1915,[39] Blanche attended Ferris Institute, where she met her future husband Bernard Coggan. While

Mrs. Marguerite Jackson, Mrs. H. L. VanDyke, Mrs. Blanche Coggan Prepare For Research Association for Michigan Negro History Dinner

Blanche Coggan (right) researching African American history.

in Lansing, she began a lifelong interest in the Michigan Underground Railroad. Scholars applauded her research:

> Her finds, according to professional historians, are nothing short of miraculous. For instance, she located the missing "Black

Books"—the original records of the Michigan Anti-Slavery society—
years after almost everybody had given them up for lost. A Pontiac
resident had them in her attic in the threadbare sewing bag that
had held them a century ago. Mrs. Coggan also has located more
than 200 underground railroad stations, including those in Lansing,
Portland, Williamston and Mason in this area. Some of the old structures are still standing.[40]

She was a founding member of the Research Association for Michigan
Negro History, and she has two paper archives: one is stored at the State
Archive of Michigan and a more extensive collection at the Charles Wright
Museum in Detroit, Michigan. In April 1957, the Michigan Legislature
referred to her as "the most extensive and prolific researcher of the
Underground Railroad in Michigan."[41]

Coggan spent her adult life dedicated to telling the history of African
Americans and Native Americans in Michigan. I am appreciative of her
work—and the motivation behind it. She was convinced that the lived
experiences of African Americans had been ignored by scholars. She
expressed this sentiment in interviews. "Almost all blacks are left out of
American history," she said, then added, "It is understandable that they
were, since many of our first histories were written by Southern men."[42]
She was right. Those first histories were written by white men, including
scholars born, reared, and shaped in the South. But that was not the only
insult to truth, later scholars, in her words, "never bothered to update
them and dig for more facts."[43]

Until recently, the collective memory of members of the Ferris
State University community did not include stories about the African
American men who came from Hampton in the first two decades of the
twentieth century. There was a time when people at Ferris Institute knew
that Gideon Smith, Belford Lawson, Percival Prattis, and other African
Americans were students here. But that knowledge was not passed on—
and later writers and tellers of our history only told the stories that they
knew. They did not follow Coggan's call to "dig for more facts." My colleague David Pilgrim and I did dig. Our hope is that others—archivists,
sociologists, and professional and amateur historians—will search for
more facts about those brave, hopeful young men and women who came
from the South to Ferris Institute and other schools in the North.

Acknowledgments

David Pilgrim

When a black person walks across a graduation stage, they owe a debt of gratitude to all of our ancestors who fought for our right to attend previously all-white schools. I am thankful for the black men featured in this book, who came north to find a college education; they and many others paved the way for me and my generation. This book is written in their honor.

It was an absolute pleasure working with Franklin Hughes, my colleague and friend. He deserves credit for unearthing this story. Thank you to David Eisler, the president of Ferris State University, who shared our enthusiasm for this project. If this book helps to rewrite existing narratives about Ferris State University—and it must!—it will be because both men understood the importance of the stories. As always, thank you to Patty Terryn, who offered editorial assistance—and patience.

Finally, I am thankful that I have a family: Margaret, Haley, Gabrielle, and Jamie.

Franklin Hughes

"In all your ways, acknowledge him. . ." First and foremost, I thank God for all he has provided and for the opportunity to tell this story. Many people on this journey shared our excitement and assisted at various points. I thank my coauthor, supervisor, and friend David Pilgrim for encouraging me to keep researching this story, for providing resources to go further, and for his tireless work on this project. I must recognize the invaluable work of Fran Rosen, who provided initial copyediting, review, and suggestions, and Michelle Rasmussen, for her recommendations and edits. Kelly McNeill provided interlibrary loan assistance. The Ferris State University archives provided scans of documents and images. Special thanks to Donzella Maupin and Andreese Scott, archivists at Hampton University, for their hospitality, professionalism, and courtesy as my wife and I researched at the Hampton campus. Finally, I express gratitude to my amazing wife Jacklyn Hughes and my family for their continued support and encouragement. I hope the impact of this story reaches all across the country and inspires people to help others rise.

Notes

First Words

1   To learn about Robert Barnum and the process of creating the mural, which was completed in 1996, see "The Visionary," Ferris State University, accessed February 1, 2020, www.ferris.edu/artwalk/08.htm.

2   The man holding the sign is believed to be Charles Raymond Hurt, a chemistry professor employed at Ferris State University for thirty-four years.

3   The core values were approved in 2007.

4   Today, this village is a municipality and has been renamed Winnsboro.

5   Caswell A. Mayo, ed., *American Druggist and Pharmaceutical Record* (New York: American Druggist Publishing Company, 1902), 58.

6   "Political Pickings," *Detroit Free Press*, November 6, 1904, 6.

7   "Colored Political Club," *Muskogee Times-Democrat*, March 15, 1912, 3.

8   Geraldine Rhoades Beckford, *Biographical Dictionary of American Physicians of African Ancestry, 1800–1920* (Cherry Hill, NJ: Africana Homestead Legacy Publishers, 2011), 255.

9   The *Tulsa Star* came into existence in 1912 as the *Muskogee Star*. It was a staunchly Democratic African American paper in an era when most African Americans aligned with the Republican Party. Andrew Jackson Smitherman, the publisher, moved the paper to Tulsa in 1913.

10 *Tulsa Star*, January 8, 1916, 4.

11 *Daily Times* (Davenport, IA), March 28, 1928, 3.

12 Year: *1880*; Census Place: *Middleport, Meigs, Ohio*; Roll: *1048*; Family History Film: *1255048*; Page: *227B*; Enumeration District: *116*.

13 Although laws forbidding whites and blacks in Ohio from marrying were overturned in 1887, interracial marriages remained socially taboo in that state and many others even after *Loving v. Virginia* (1967), the landmark Supreme Court decision that invalidated anti-miscegenation laws in all states.

14 In 1872, when Fowler was only fourteen years old, he was the only black player on a professional team in New Castle, Pennsylvania. On April 24, 1878, he pitched in a game for the Picked Nine against the Boston Red Caps, champions of the National League in 1877. The Picked Nine won the game. To gain insight into the

Negro Leagues, see Robert Peterson, *Only the Ball Was White: A History of Legendary Black Players and All-Black Professional Teams* (New York: Oxford University Press, 1992).

15 "Will Play Ball Again," *Big Rapids Pioneer*, July 24, 1902, 3.

16 To learn more about Foster, see Larry Lester, *Rube Foster in His Time: On the Field and in the Papers with Black Baseball's Greatest Visionary* (Jefferson, NC: McFarland and Co., 2012).

17 "Big Rapids Giants Win," *Big Rapids Pioneer*, August 21, 1902, 3.

18 The first official championship was the 1924 Colored World Series, a match-up between the Kansas City Monarchs, from the Negro National League, and the Hilldale Athletic Club, the Eastern Colored League champions. In a ten-game series, the Monarchs defeated Hilldale five games to four, with one game ending in a tie.

19 The Cubs finished second in the National League, six and a half games behind the Pittsburgh Pirates. The team had won the pennant the previous three years and would win it again in 1910. The Cubs were led by the legendary Joe Tinker, Johnny Evers, and Frank Chance.

20 "The Chicago Giants Base Ball Club," *Chicago Defender*, January 22, 1910, 1.

21 *Pittsburgh Courier*, February 25, 1933, 14.

22 Harry Daniels, "The Base Ball Spirit in the East," *Indianapolis Freeman*, December 25, 1909, 7.

23 The Grays team included Smokey Joe Williams, elected to the Major League Baseball Hall of Fame in 1999.

24 "Nate Harris Aids Grays in Training," *Pittsburgh Courier*, April 18, 1925, 12.

25 It is unclear if he enrolled at Ferris in 1902. The university archives has an enrollment card for him for the 1903 academic term.

26 "The Would-Be Champions Downed," *Big Rapids Pioneer*, November 25, 1902, 3.

27 "Ferris Is in Favor: Faculty of Ferris Institute, Big Rapids, Adopts Football," *Grand Rapids Herald*, September 4, 1903, 10.

28 Ibid.

29 Ibid.

30 "Home Team Won—10 to 0," *Traverse City (MI) Evening Record*, October 3, 1903, 4.

31 "Ferris Team Never in It," *Detroit Free Press*, October 22, 1903, 3.

32 Grif Stockley, *Ruled by Race: Black/White Relations in Arkansas from Slavery to the Present* (Fayetteville: University of Arkansas Press, 2012), 95.

33 Aldridge Edward Bush and P.L. Dorman, *History of the Mosaic Templars of America: Its Founders and Officials* (Fayetteville: University of Arkansas Press, 2008), 179.

34 See Booker T. Washington, *The Negro in Business* (Boston: Hertel, Jenkins and Co., 1907). Washington explains the origins of the National Negro Business League and highlights many successful entrepreneurs, including John Bush and E.E. McDaniel.

35 Cyril H. McAdam, "Booker T. Washington's Recent Trip through the Southwest," *Colored American Magazine*, January 1906, 35.

36 E.M. Woods, *Blue Book of Little Rock and Argenta, Arkansas* (Little Rock: Central Printing Co., 1907), 121.

37 "Newspaper Men and Leaders in Important Conference: Discuss Ways to Best Help Nation Win the War; Personnel of Gathering," *Chicago Defender*, July 6, 1918, 4.

38   "Progress of the Race in Our Sister State," *Topeka Plaindealer*, June 9, 1916, 2.

39   "Editor Chiles Tells of Race Progress in His Travels thru Missouri and Kansas," *Topeka Plaindealer*, November 18, 1921, 1.

40   "Through Missouri with the Editor," *Topeka Plaindealer*, August 10, 1923, 1.

41   Personal correspondence with Linda Jones, vice president of the Annie Malone Historical Society, December 3, 2018.

42   Gideon Smith is shown three times in the 1911 yearbook: in the senior class roll, with the Ferris Institute band, and with the football team. In 1912, there is only one picture of Smith: in a photograph of the football team, his left hand resting comfortably on the shoulder of a white teammate.

43   Gregory Bond, "Jim Crow at Play: Race, Manliness, and the Color Line in American Sports, 1876–1916," (PhD diss., University of Wisconsin-Madison, 2008), 440.

44   Charles H. Martin, "The Color Line in Midwestern Sport 1890–1960," *Indiana Magazine of History*, June 2002, 98–99.

45   "Area Deaths and Funerals," *Newport News Daily Press*, September 12, 1974, 17.

46   Harry Munford was joined at Ferris by Arthur James Wells and Walter N. Lowe in 1916. In the 1917 *Crimson and Gold*, there are pictures labeled as "Snapshots." One of the snapshots includes an image of Walter Lowe on the left, Arthur Wells on the right, and Harry Munford in the middle, with his arms on the shoulders of his two classmates.

47   "Michigan Board," *Druggist Circular* 61 (1917): 314.

48   *Records of the Office of the Quartermaster General, 1774–1985*, Record Group Number 92, Roll or Box Number: *337*; National Archives at College Park, College Park, MD.

49   Hampton Normal and Agricultural Institute became simply Hampton Institute in 1930. With the addition of departments and graduate programs, it was accredited as Hampton University in 1984.

50   Percival Prattis, "Changing Years," from an unpublished autobiographical manuscript, 85. Manuscript access courtesy of Patricia Prattis Jennings, later donated to Percival L. Prattis Papers, 1916–1980, AIS.2007.01, Archives Service Center, University of Pittsburgh, Series 1 Subseries 4: Writings, Box 2, Folder 85.

51   A handful of the Hampton students came to Ferris to take business courses. Grady Herring was from Lamar, Alabama. He was a business student at Hampton in 1920–1921. From 1922 to 1924, Herring was enrolled in the college preparatory program at the Ferris Institute. In the 1925 catalog, Herring was listed as enrolled in the Commercial Department.

52   His name is sometimes written as Maceo Richard Clark.

53   Belford Lawson was also on the baseball team in 1919. Clarke is one of four African Americans in a 1919 picture of the baseball team. Woodbridge Ferris is also in the photograph.

54   The Washington Potomacs operated as an independent baseball team in 1923. The next year they joined the Eastern Colored League, based in Washington, DC. In 1925, the Potomacs moved to Wilmington, Delaware, and played as the Wilmington Potomacs.

55   Benjamin Harris Taylor (1888–1953) played for the Birmingham Giants, Chicago American Giants, Indianapolis ABCs, St. Louis Giants, Bacharach Giants, Washington Potomacs, Harrisburg Giants, and Baltimore Black Sox.

56   The 1900 U.S. Census lists Walter, Maceo, and Hannibal as the sons of Richard and Alice Clark (Clarke). In 1900, Walter is listed as four years old, Maceo as two

years old, and Hannibal as seven months old. Their father Richard was a teacher at a public school in Chatham, Virginia.

57 Office of University Relations, "MU NewsLetter, November 16, 1995," *MU NewsLetter 1987–1999*, Paper 290, accessed February 1, 2020, http://mds.marshall.edu/oldmu_newsletter/290.

58 Isabel Wilkerson, *The Warmth of Other Suns: The Epic Story of America's Great Migration* (New York: Random House, 2010). This book chronicles the decades-long migration of black people who fled the South for northern and western cities.

59 Joe William Trotter, *The African American Experience* (Boston: Houghton Mifflin, 2001), 378.

60 Jan Voogd, *Race Riots and Resistance: The Red Summer of 1919* (New York: Peter Lang, 2008). This book documents the number of incidents and describes the events in detail. Also see Cameron McWhirter, *Red Summer: The Summer of 1919 and the Awakening of Black America* (New York: Henry Holt and Co., 2011).

61 Many newspapers carried this erroneous assertion; for example, the *Wilmington (DE) Morning News*, May 12, 1919, stated, "The trouble was said to have grown out of the shooting of a sailor by a Negro in a downtown poolroom."

62 "Quiet Follows Charleston Riot," *Greenville (SC) News*, May 12, 1919, 1. This newspaper also made the erroneous claim about the riot's origins: "The police however, say that according to the best information they have been able to obtain the rioting was precipitated when the negro Isaac Doctor was fatally wounded after he had shot a sailor."

63 "Six Killed and Many Wounded in Charleston Riot," *Greenville (SC) News*, May 11, 1919, 1.

64 "Chicago Riots Sickened Him," *Concordia (KS) Blade-Empire*, August 2, 1919, 1.

65 "Black Invasion of Whites' Beach Causes Trouble," *Daily Republican-Register* (Mount Carmel, Illinois), July 28, 1919, 1.

66 Nikki L.M. Brown and Barry M. Stentiford, *The Jim Crow Encyclopedia: Greenwood Milestones in African American History* (Westport, CT: Greenwood Publishing Group, 2008), 128.

67 Chad L. Williams, *Torchbearers of Democracy: African American Soldiers in the World War I Era* (Chapel Hill: University of North Carolina Press, 2010).

68 Richard Slotkin, *Lost Battalions: The Great War and the Crisis of American Nationality* (New York: Henry Holt and Co., 2005), 235.

69 Tom Shanahan, *Raye of Light: Jimmy Raye, Duffy Daugherty, the Integration of College Football, and the 1965–66 Michigan State Spartans* (Middleton, WI: August Publications, 2014), 57; Booker T. Washington, *Up from Slavery* (New York: Dover Publications, 1995 [1901]).

70 There were other African American men pictured in the *Crimson and Gold* yearbooks that covered the 1910 to 1928 period; however, we have been unable to determine if they had attended Hampton.

71 Tom Shanahan's comments were delivered at a book signing on November 6, 2014, at Ferris State University.

72 George Newman Fuller and Lewis Beeson, *Michigan History*, vol. 1 (Charleston, SC: Nabu Press, 2010 [1917]), 33.

Making the World Better: Woodbridge Ferris

1   This was the pre–residential halls days. Students attending Ferris Institute had to find accommodations in rooming houses.
2   "Address of Gov. Woodbridge N. Ferris," in Francis H. Warren, *Michigan Manual of Freedmen's Progress* (Detroit: Michigan Freedmen's Progress Commission, 1915), 365.
3   "Big Rapids Fire Perils Students," *Lansing State Journal*, November 22, 1926, 1.
4   "Lives on Old Homestead," *Calumet (MI) News*, December 30, 1912, 2. The article mentions that Estella Ferris was still living in a family cabin when Woodbridge was elected governor of Michigan. This is disputed by a different article, which claimed that Ferris's mother and sister Olive lived "near the old homestead on which the Governor was born"; "Gov. Ferris's Mother Lives in Halsey Valley," *The Ithaca (NY) Journal*, October 19, 1916, 6.
5   "Ferris Institute to Fete Founder's 100th Birthday," *Lansing State Journal*, December 27, 1952, 3.
6   Woodbridge N. Ferris, *The Autobiography of Woodbridge N. Ferris* (Big Rapids, MI: Ferris State University, 1995), 60.
7   Ibid., 61.
8   Ibid., 62.
9   "Silas W. Brewster—Early Hannibal Merchant and Abolitionist," Oswego Historical Society, accessed February 13, 2020, http://rbhousemuseum.org/wp-content/uploads/2017/06/SBrewsterMerchantAbolotionist-1.pdf.
10   "John P. and Lydia Edwards House," National Park Service U.S. Department of the Interior, accessed February 13, 2020, www.nps.gov/nr/travel/underground/Edwards_house.html.
11   The authors recommend a recent biography of Frederick Douglass: David W. Bright, *Frederick Douglass: Prophet of Freedom* (New York: Simon and Schuster, 2018).
12   "Anti-Slavery Excursion to Cape Cod," *The Liberator* (Boston, MA), July 1, 1842, 2.
13   Frederick Douglass, *Narrative of the Life of Frederick Douglass, an American Slave* (Boston: Anti-slavery Office, 1845), accessed February 1, 2020, www.ibiblio.org/ebooks/Douglass/Narrative/Douglass_Narrative.pdf; reprinted numerous times, in 2020, the book remained a best-selling memoir on Amazon.
14   "England and America," *Manchester (UK) Weekly Times and Examiner*, March 21, 1846.
15   Black people were re-enslaved as late as the 1940s through a system of peonage; see Douglas A. Blackmon, *Slavery by Another Name: The Re-Enslavement of Black Americans from the Civil War to World War II* (London: Icon, 2012).
16   *Useful Education* (Ferris Industrial), 1895, 3.
17   W.N. Ferris, "The Courage That Conquers," *The Journal of Commercial Education* 19 (1902): 57–59.
18   W.E.B. Du Bois, *The Souls of Black Folk* (Oxford: Oxford University Press, 2007 [1903]).
19   "Address of Gov. Ferris," *Michigan Manual*, 368–69.
20   "Negro Lynched by an Angry Mob," *Pittsburgh Press*, July 17, 1902, 1.
21   "Negro Burned," *Mattoon (IL) Daily Journal*, July 17, 1902, 7.
22   "Burned at a Stake: A Negro Brute Gets What He Deserved," *Robesonian* (Lumberton, NC), July 22, 1902, 1.

23 "Burned at Stake by Mississippi Mob: Swift and Terrible Vengeance for Negro's Crime," *Washington (DC) Evening Times*, July 17, 1902, 1.

24 Ibid.

25 There are many well-researched books about lynching, e.g., see Philip Dray, *At the Hands of Persons Unknown: The Lynching of Black America* (New York: Modern Library, 2003); Equal Justice Initiative, *Lynching in America: Confronting the Legacy of Racial Terror* (Montgomery, AL: Equal Justice Initiative, 2015).

26 "Negro Burned at a Stake," *Wilmington (DE) News Journal*, July 17, 1902, 1.

27 "Mob Burns Negro to Death," *New York Sun*, July 18, 1902, 10.

28 "A Magnificent Gathering: Booker T. Washington Received a Warm Greeting in Big Rapids," *Big Rapids Pioneer*, July 17, 1902, 3.

29 Booker T. Washington, *Up from Slavery* (New York: Dover Publications, 1995 [1901]), 1.

30 Later, his mother told him that she had named him "Booker Taliaferro" at his birth, but neither he nor others used Taliaferro. After learning of his birth name, Washington readopted it, and for the rest of his life he was known as Booker Taliaferro Washington.

31 Washington, *Up from Slavery*, 53. Tuskegee Institute opened three years before Ferris Institute.

32 "A Magnificent Gathering," 3.

33 Ralph McGill, "W.E.B. Du Bois," *Atlantic Monthly*, November 1965, accessed February 1, 2020, http://www.theatlantic.com/past/docs/unbound/flashbks/black/mcgillbh.htm.

34 Benjamin Ryan Tillman served as Governor of South Carolina from 1890 to 1894 and as a United States Senator from 1895 until his death in 1918. He led a paramilitary group of Red Shirts during South Carolina's violent 1876 election. On the floor of the U.S. Senate, he ridiculed black people and boasted of having helped kill them. One of his legacies was South Carolina's 1895 constitution, which disenfranchised most of the black majority and ensured white supremacy for more than half a century.

35 "The Era of Blease," *Charlotte Observer*, March 4, 1912, 4. Coleman Livingston Blease also served as the ninetieth governor of South Carolina (1910–1912).

36 "Booker T. Washington Delivers the 1895 Atlanta Compromise Speech," History Matters, accessed February 1, 2020, http://historymatters.gmu.edu/d/39.

37 "Southern Resentment: Aroused by Booker Washington's Presence at President's Table," *Washington DC Evening Star*, October 18, 1901, 12.

38 Ibid.

39 "Brutal Politics," *St. Joseph (MO) Gazette-Herald*, November 4, 1901, 4.

40 "Roosevelt Roasted: Democratic Press Denouncing Him for Entertaining Booker Washington at the White House," *Jackson Clarion-Ledger*, October 21, 1901, 6.

41 To read the poem, see "Niggers in the White House," *Austin American-Statesman*, February 11, 1902, 4. The poem reappeared in 1929 in response to Jesse L. (Williams) De Priest, an African American, eating in the White House via an invitation by First Lady Lou Henry Hoover, wife of President Herbert Hoover.

42 "Why Take a Boy from His Walk," *Ogden Standard*, December 30, 1908, 7.

43 After his death, Woodbridge's copy of the book was donated to Ferris Institute; however, the book, which included handwritten notes by Woodbridge, has been lost.

44   Kenneth M. Hamilton, *Booker T. Washington in American Memory* (Urbana: University of Illinois Press, 2017), 172.

45   Franz Joseph Gall initially called his theory cranioscopy. His colleague Johann Spurzheim coined the term *phrenology*.

46   Margarita Tartakovsky, "Phrenology: Examining the Bumps of Your Brain," Psych Central, July, 2018, accessed February 13, 2020, psychcentral.com/blog/phrenology-examining-the-bumps-of-your-brain.

47   Martin Staum, *Labeling People: French Scholars on Society, Race and Empire, 1815–1848* (Montreal: McGill-Queen's University Press, 2003), 59.

48   James Poskett, "Django Unchained and the Racist Science of Phrenology," *Guardian*, February 5, 2013, accessed February 13, 2020, www.theguardian.com/science/blog/2013/feb/05/django-unchained-racist-science-phrenology.

49   Woodbridge N. Ferris, "Work Together," *Ann Arbor Negro Year Book, 1918*, 151.

50   "Local University Closes Another Successful Year," *Valparaiso (IN) Porter County Vidette*, August 22, 1917, 7.

51   "Lecture at High School," *Bessemer (MI) Herald*, September 30, 1899, 5.

52   "Michigan Senator Is among Speakers," *Rushville (IN) Daily Republican*, July 31, 1925, 1.

53   George Newman Fuller and Lewis Beeson, *Michigan History*, vol. 1 (Charleston, SC: Nabu Press, 2010 [1917]), 34.

54   "Ferris Gives Address at Banquet in Berrien," *Detroit Free Press*, February 13, 1923, 23.

55   Arthur H. Vanderberg, *The Greatest American, Alexander Hamilton: An Historical Analysis of His Life and Works Together with a Symposium of Opinions by Distinguished Americans* (New York: G.P Putnam's Sons, 1922), 17–18.

56   "The Ferris Lecture," *Port Huron Times Herald*, March 13, 1907, 6.

57   "Class Completes W.B.C. Studies," *Waterloo (IA) Courier*, February 25, 1910, 7. This newspaper article provides excerpts from and a favorable critique of Woodbridge Ferris's speech.

58   *St. Joseph (MI) Saturday Herald*, November 19, 1904, 4. This article includes an assessment of Ferris as an educator, a man, and a prospective politician: "When every student speaks good words for the teacher, like those who have attended at the Ferris Institute and utter them for W.N. Ferris, others need have no cause to regret the good word and support given to such a man before and on election day. Mr. Ferris is not a politician but an every day honorable, pleasing citizen whom one delights to meet and counsel with."

59   Willis F. Dunbar and George S. May, *Michigan: A History of the Wolverine State* (Grand Rapids, MI: Wm. B. Eerdmans Publishing Co., 1995), 452.

60   Agassiz Association, *The Guide to Nature* 10, no. 1 (1917): 125.

61   Caryn Hannan, *Michigan Biographical Dictionary* (Hamburg, MI: State History Publications, 1998), 234.

62   Jay W. Forrest and James Malcolm, *Tammany's Treason, Impeachment of Governor Williams Sulzer: The Complete Story Written from Behind the Scenes, Showing How Tammany Plays the Game, How Men Are Bought, Sold and Delivered* (Albany, NY: Fort Orange Press, 1913), 439.

63   Randall Maurice Jelks, *African Americans in the Furniture City: The Struggle for Civil Rights in Grand Rapids* (Urbana: University of Illinois Press, 2016), 25.

64   Ibid.

65   Francis H. Warren, The Michigan Manual of Freedmen's Progress (Detroit: Freedmen's Progress Commission, 1915), accessed February 22, 2020, https://www.library.wmich.edu/digidb/freedmen/content/EXWA_freedmen.pdf.

66   "Black Michigan: How They Met the Challenge," Detroit Free Press, February 2, 1986, 21.

67   "The Lincoln Jubilee and Fifty Years of Freedom Celebration Is Now Running at Full Blast at the Coliseum and Will Continue Each Day until September 16th," The Broad Ax (Chicago, IL), August 28, 1915. This article gives a detailed description of the events each day at the Jubilee celebration.

68   D.W. Griffith, Birth of a Nation (Universal City, CA: Epoch Producing Co., 1915).

69   Thomas Dixon, The Clansman: An Historical Romance of the Ku Klux Klan (New York: Grosset and Dunlop, 1905).

70   "Willis' Decision Upheld," Fulton County Tribune (Wauseon, OH), March 24, 1916, 3.

71   Michigan Historical Collections (Lansing, MI: Wynkoop Hallenbeck Crawford, Co., 1914), 276.

72   "Senator Ferris of Michigan, Dies from Pneumonia," Olean (NY) Times Herald, March 23, 1928, 1.

73   The bid failed, John W. Davis was nominated—he lost the election to Calvin Coolidge.

74   "Senator Ferris Nominated as Most Fitting for Leader," Philadelphia Inquirer, June 27, 1924, 14. Ferris received thirty votes on the first ballot, which placed his candidacy in eighth place. His delegates turned to other candidates.

75   "U.S. Senator to Talk at 5th St.," Harrisburg (PA) Evening News, January 27, 1923, 4. When the author wrote "champion of the right," this was not a reference to political camps but to being "morally right."

76   "Senator Ferris Tells of Trip to Hampton, VA," Ferris Institute News, February 21, 1928, 1–2. This was likely his last public speech.

77   Ibid., 2.

78   Ferris, "Work Together," 151.

79   "Brochial Pneumonia Causes Death Friday of Michigan Solon," Franklin (IN) Evening Star, March 23, 1928, 1.

80   "Prophet of Virtues," Benton Harbor News-Palladium, March 27, 1928, 8.

81   "Michigan G.O.P. and Democrat Leaders Split on Vandenberg," Baltimore Afro-American, October 7, 1939, 8.

Ready to Play: Gideon Smith

1   Steve Grinczel, Michigan State Football: They Are Spartans (Charleston, SC: Arcadia Publishing, 2004), 17.

2   An article in Jet magazine said that Smith was "generally regarded as one of the toughest linemen in Midwest football history"; "Reunion for Old Aggies," Jet, November 12, 1953, 56.

3   "Marquette No Match for Aggies," Detroit Free Press, November 7, 1915, 22.

4   He was also referred to as G.E. Smith, Gid Smith, Charlie Smith, and George Brown.

5   The 1900 Census lists Patience and her children, including Gideon, as "black," the 1910 Census designated each family member as "mulatto," but the 1920 Census again lists them as "black."

6   The household included Wilson's sister, Annie M., thirty-nine; nephew, Hugh G., fifteen; and niece, Nina, eleven.

7   1900: Census Place: *Pleasant Grove, Norfolk, Virginia*; Roll: 1719; Page: 7B; Enumeration District: 0037; FHL microfilm: 1241719.

8   Personal Letter from Gideon Smith to "Dear Friend," written on February 25, 1907.

9   Ibid.

10 "Graduates and Ex-Students," *Southern Workman*, November 1910, 641.

11 *Crimson and Gold* (Big Rapids, MI: Ferris Institute, 1911), 22.

12 *Crimson and Gold* (Big Rapids, MI: Ferris Institute, 1910), 96.

13 Marc Sheehan, *Ferris State University: The First 125 Years* (St. Louis: Reedy Press, 2009), 60.

14 Taggart is in the Ferris State University Bulldog Athletics Hall of Fame, and the current football team plays on Top Taggart Field. Nate Harris was the coach of the football team in 1902–1903.

15 "F.I. Team Bests Grand Haven: First Game of the Season Seen by Large Crowd," *Big Rapids Pioneer*, October 10, 1910, 1.

16 *Big Rapids Pioneer*, October 21, 1911, 1.

17 "Scrubs Put Up Strong Battle," *Lansing State Journal*, November 25, 1912, 8.

18 "Cobb, Star Booter in M.A.C. Ranks, First to Receive Injury," *Lansing State Journal*, September 23, 1913, 8.

19 "M.A.C. Beats Crimson in First Game of New Season," *The M.A.C. Record*, October 7, 1913, 1.

20 "Aggies Defeat Olivet Saturday 26 to 0 in First Game of Season," *Lansing State Journal*, October 6, 1913, 8.

21 "Alma Takes Bad Beating from Macklin's Warriors," *The M.A.C. Record*, October 14, 1913, 3.

22 "M.A.C. Humbles Michigan: Macklin's Men Outplay and Defeat Maize and Blue in Wonderful Struggle," *The M.A.C. Record*, October 21, 1913, 1.

23 "Michigan Agricultural College Eleven Achieves Great Victory: Yost's Men Bowed to Superior Team," *Lansing State Journal*, October 20, 1913, 5.

24 A decade earlier, the University of Wisconsin threatened to forfeit a game against the University of Kansas, because the latter had a black player; "Race Line in Football and Military," *Minneapolis Journal*, October 14, 1903, 4.

25 "Michigan Aggies Have Best Claim to Western Title," *Lansing State Journal*, October 27, 1913, 8. Bob Butler was elected to the College Football Hall of Fame in 1972.

26 "Smith, the Negro Tackle," *The New York Age*, February 12, 1914, 6.

27 "Letter Sent to Colored Tackle by Gov. Ferris, "*Lansing State Journal*, October 31, 1913, 9.

28 "Pioneers," *Lansing State Journal*, February 16, 1988, 23.

29 John Matthew Smith, "Black Power in Green and White: Integration and Black Protest in Michigan State University Football, 1947–1972" (master's thesis, Western Michigan University, 2006), 20–21.

30 Steve Grinczel, "Celebrating the Legacy of Gideon Smith," Michigan State: The Official Website of Spartan Athletics, accessed February 3, 2020, msuspartans.com/news/2013/10/15/Celebrating_the_Legacy_of_Gideon_Smith.aspx.

31 "Showed Nerve When His Nose Was Broken," *Lansing State Journal*, October 22, 1912, 8.

32   "Julian Took Player Up Fire Escape," *Akron Beacon Journal*, December 1, 1915, 12.

33   Ibid.

34   John Milton Belcher III, Gideon's grandson, remembered him as a gentle man. Private communication between Belcher and the researchers, November 7, 2017.

35   Oceania Chalk, *Pioneers of Black Sport: The Early Days of the Black Professional Athlete in Baseball, Basketball, Boxing, and Football* (New York: Dodd Mead, 1975), 214.

36   "Five of Macklin's Veterans Play Final Games Saturday," *The Fort Wayne Journal-Gazette*, November 5, 1915, 22.

37   "East Is Niggardly; Aggies Turn to West for Football Games," *Lansing State Journal*, February 19, 1916, 6.

38   "Negro Didn't Need Any Head Guard," *Akron Beacon Journal*, October 18, 1913, 12.

39   "Attention, Alabam'," *The Daily Missoulian*, October 22, 1913, 5.

40   "Smith Will Be Banqueted at African M.E. Church," *Lansing State Journal*, December 5, 1913, 8.

41   "Dusky Tackle Up in Ranks of Race; Football His Sport," *Canton Daily News*, December 14, 1913, 24.

42   "Sidelights on the Wolverine Victory," *Detroit Free Press*, October 18, 1914, 19.

43   "Fumbling Mars Win of Aggies," *Detroit Free Press*, October 17, 1915, 23.

44   "M.A.C. Smothers Michigan under a Score of 24 to 0," *Detroit Free Press*, October 24, 1915, 19.

45   Ibid., 19, 23.

46   "The Sport Grist by George S. Alderson: Thirty Years Ago," *Lansing State Journal*, April 11, 1947, 21.

47   Marion Motley and Bill Willis signed with the Cleveland Browns of the All-America Football Conference and Kenny Washington and Woody Strode signed with the National Football League's Los Angeles Rams.

48   "Wendell Smith's Sports Beat," *Pittsburgh Courier*, November 1, 1958, 21.

49   "Dr. Hill Keeps Busy," *Newport News Daily Press*, September 27, 1984, 87.

A Relentless Foe: Belford Lawson

1   Ellis L. (sometimes Ellie) Herring was another Ferris/Hampton student who became an attorney. He was a college preparatory student at Ferris from 1922 to 1925, then attended Detroit City College (now Wayne State University). He practiced law in Detroit and hosted Detroit-Hampton club meetings in the 1930s in his home. Oakes Ames White, from Retz, Virginia, attended the Hampton Institute before enrolling in Ferris's college preparatory program in 1923. He was a stellar member of the debating club at Ferris, before moving on to study law at Detroit City College, where he was "the only colored student who has taken first place in an oratorical contest or made the varsity debating team"; see *Southern Workman*, 1930, 476.

2   Belford Lawson III (Belford Lawson's son) in telephone interview with authors, April 2018.

3   Ibid.

4   *Ferris Institute Catalog* (Big Rapids, MI: Ferris Institute, 1920), 127.

5   "Hope Swamps Ferris Nine at Big Rapids," *Holland (MI) Anchor*, May 12, 1920, 1. In this newspaper account, Clark's entry as a pitcher was described this way: "Clark the dusky southpaw was substituted, but color made no difference for they

all looked alike to Hope." The writer was suggesting that the Hope batters had success against all the Ferris pitchers.

6   "College Inflicts Terrific Deluge on Institutors," *Holland (MI) Anchor*, November 12, 1919, 1.

7   Ibid.

8   Letter written by Belford Lawson to Myrilla J. Sherman, the Hampton registrar, September 9, 1919.

9   "Negro Halfback Wins Oratorical Honors," *Bloomington (IL) Pentagraph*, May 1923, 12.

10   "'Leave Town,' Says Alleged Letter of Klan to Student," *Michigan Daily*, January 17, 1924, 1. Lyman J. Glasgow, a white student, also received a letter. These words were included, "Our advice to you is to leave Ann Arbor now as a result of unfriendly things you have said concerning the K.K.K. Leave now while your friends know where you are. Expecting to see you gone in a month."

11   Ibid.

12   Charles C. Teamer, "A Distinguished Fraternal Leader," *Sphinx*, 1985, 24.

13   "Fraternity to Celebrate Founder's Day," *Annapolis Capital*, February 8, 1964, 3.

14   "Reserves Hold Varsity Linemen in Disappointing Scrimmage," *Michigan Daily*, October 1, 1922, 6.

15   "Reserves Score! Happiness Rules," *Michigan Daily*, October 5, 1922, 7.

16   "Reserves Win Game from Freshmen, 3–0," *Michigan Daily*, October 14, 1922, 6.

17   "Goebel's Cohorts Down Gladiators," *Michigan Daily*, May 5, 1923, 6.

18   Yost coached at Michigan from 1901 through 1923, and again in 1925 and 1926. After retiring from coaching, he became the university's athletic director, a position he held until 1940.

19   Nicholas J. Cotsonika, *Century of Champions* (Detroit: Detroit Free Press, 1999), 41.

20   Joe Falls, Bob Wojnowski, and John U. Bacon, *A Legacy of Champions: The Story of the Men Who Built University of Michigan Football* (Farmington Hills, MI: CTC Productions and Sports, 1996), 65.

21   Paul E. Brown, Lopez D. Matthews Jr., Frederick Nickens IV, and Ronald Anthony Mills Sr., *The History of Alpha Phi Alpha: Origins of the Eastern Region* (Baltimore: Foundation Publishers, 2017), 22.

22   Kenneth Robert Janken, *Rayford W. Logan and the Dilemma of the African-American Intellectual* (Amherst: University of Massachusetts Press, 1997), 99.

23   Gregory Parks, ed., *Black Greek-Letter Organizations in the Twenty-First Century: Our Fight Has Just Begun* (Lexington: University Press of Kentucky, 2008), 148.

24   The *Sphinx* was a valuable research tool for this project. Many of the men in this book were leaders in local fraternity chapters, and their activities were reported in the *Sphinx*.

25   "Doings During the Eastern Regional," *Sphinx*, May–June 1973, 32.

26   Gregory Parks and Stefan M. Bradley, *Alpha Phi Alpha: A Legacy of Greatness, the Demands of Transcendence* (Lexington: University of Kentucky Press, 2012), 126.

27   "Morris Brown Gridders at Hard Practice," *Pittsburgh Courier*, October 3, 1925, 15.

28   *Pittsburgh Courier*, April 20, 1929, 14. Presumably, this meant that he had both white and black clients.

29   Theodore Moody Berry served as president of the Cincinnati chapter of the NAACP from 1932 to 1938. He also served on the NAACP National Board of Directors from 1946 to 1965.

30 "Our History," Howard University School of Law, accessed February 3, 2020, http://law.howard.edu/content/our-history.

31 Wilbur C. Rich, ed., *African American Perspectives on Political Science* (Philadelphia: Temple University Press, 2007), 171.

32 *New Negro Alliance v. Sanitary Grocery Co.* (1938), accessed February 3, 2020, caselaw. findlaw.com/us-supreme-court/303/552.html.

33 Michele F. Pacifico, "Don't Buy Where You Can't Work: The New Negro Alliance of Washington," *Washington History,* Spring–Summer 1994, 86–88.

34 Mark V. Tushnet, *Making Civil Rights Law: Thurgood Marshall and the Supreme Court, 1936–1961* (New York: Oxford University Press, 1996), 136.

35 Joan Quigley, *Just Another Southern Town: Mary Church Terrell and the Struggle for Racial Justice in the Nation's Capital* (New York: Oxford University Press, 2016), 146.

36 Ibid.

37 Richard Kluger, *Simple Justice: The History of Brown v. Board of Education and Black America's Struggle for Equality* (New York: Knopf, 1976), 276.

38 The chief arguments in this case were made by Lawson. Lawyers appearing for Henderson were Jawn Sandifer, Marjorie M. McKenzie, Sydney A. Jones Jr., Earl B. Dickerson, Josiah F. Henry Jr., Charlotte R. Pinkett, Aubrey E. Robinson Jr., Edward W. Brooke, William M. McClain, Theodore M. Berry, and George Windsor.

39 "Attorney General Appeals to Supreme Court to Tear Down Segregation Barriers in U.S." *Delta Democrat-Times* (Greenville, Mississippi), April 4, 1950, 2.

40 "Southern Is Accused of Segregation," *Kannapolis (NC) Daily Independent,* November 13, 1950, 1.

41 "Lawson Sees Hand of God as Dooming Segregation: 'Separate but Equal' Faces Destruction, Says Alpha Prexy," *Pittsburgh Courier,* May 5, 1951, 18.

42 Ibid.

43 "Talk O' Town," *Pittsburgh Courier,* November 5, 1938, 9.

44 "Marjorie McKenzie Lawson," *The Washington Post,* October 16, 2002, accessed February 3, 2020, www.washingtonpost.com/archive/local/2002/10/16/marjorie-mckenzie-lawson/9315feda-77f1-4ebb-a94e-9f71663c757c/?utm_term=.52cd99b28de1.

45 The black vote was critical to Kennedy—he won the black vote by a seventy to thirty margin; in the popular vote, Kennedy's margin of victory was among the closest in American history.

46 Belford V. Lawson, interview recorded by Ronald J. Grele, January 11, 1966, 2–3, John F. Kennedy Library Oral History Program.

47 Ibid., 2.

48 Earl Ofari Hutchinson, "JFK's Civil Rights Legacy: 50 Years of Myth and Fact," *HuffPost,* January 23, 2014, accessed February 5, 2020, www.huffingtonpost.com/earl-ofari-hutchinson/jfks-civil-rights-legacy_b_4290163.html.

49 Lawson, Oral History, 5

50 Ibid., 15.

51 "Will Blacks Swallow the Elephant," *The Greenwood (MI) Commonwealth,* September 19, 2004, 4.

52 Carl Skutsch, *Encyclopedia of the World's Minorities* (Hoboken: Taylor and Francis, 2013), 709.

53 To read the full transcript, see John F. Kennedy, "Televised Address to the Nation on Civil Rights," John F. Kennedy Presidential Library and Museum, accessed

February 5, 2020, www.jfklibrary.org/learn/about-jfk/historic-speeches/televised-address-to-the-nation-on-civil-rights.

54   The legislation was coauthored with Walter Mondale, a Minnesota Democrat and colleague on the Senate Banking Committee. President Lyndon B. Johnson signed the bill into law one week after the assassination of Martin Luther King Jr.

55   *Baltimore Afro American*, November 1, 1966, 7.

56   Frankie Muse Freeman, *A Song of Faith and Hope: The Life of Frankie Muse Freeman* (St. Louis: Missouri Historical Society Press, 2003), 42.

57   Houston A. Baker, *Betrayal: How Black Intellectuals Have Abandoned the Ideals of the Civil Rights Era* (New York: Columbia University Press, 2010), 9.

58   "Baltimorean Wins Award at Amherst," *Baltimore Evening Sun*, June 2, 1934, 16.

59   Juan Williams, *Thurgood Marshall: American Revolutionary* (New York: Times Books, 1998), 76. Williams apparently did not know about Lawson's role.

60   "200 At Dinner Honor Pastor of Faith Church," *Hartford Courant*, March 11, 1956, 36.

61   "Lawson to Speak at 'Y' Sunday," *Pittsburgh Courier*, March 16, 1935, 1.

62   David L. Lewis, *W.E.B. Du Bois: A Biography* (New York: Henry Holt and Co., 2009), 692.

63   "Timmerman Walks Out on Lawson!" *Pittsburgh Courier*, August 18, 1956, 4.

64   As a child, Lawson was excluded from the local YMCA.

65   District of Columbia, Board of Commissioners, Resolution to honor Belford Lawson, Jr., March 26, 1985, retrieved from District of Columbia Register.

66   "Frat Head Hits Southern Revolt," *Baltimore Sun*, March 8, 1948, 7.

67   "Slogans Stymie Civil Rights Gains, Says Washington Negro Attorney," *Jefferson City Post-Tribune*, February 27, 1967, 3.

Race News: African American Journalists

1   The Freedmen's Bureau had stopped its financial support.

2   "Christiansburg Institute," Montgomery Museum and Lewis Miller Regional Art Center, accessed February 5, 2020, montgomerymuseum.org/learn/historic-christiansburg-walking-tour/christiansburg-institute.

3   Percival Prattis, unpublished autobiographical manuscript, 85, access to the manuscript courtesy of Patricia Prattis Jennings, later donated to Percival L. Prattis Papers, 1916–1980, AIS.2007.01, Archives Service Center, University of Pittsburgh, Series 1 Subseries 4: Writings, Box 2, Folder 85. We found two sections that may be chapters, though the pagination suggests otherwise. The quote above is from "Changing Years," 20. There is another section called "Nonsense." We will treat them as if they were chapters to be included in a single manuscript.

4   Ibid., 22.

5   Ibid., 41.

6   "Graduates and Ex-Students," *Southern Workman*, September 1918, 462.

7   Charles A. Rosenberg, "Percival L. Prattis: The Pittsburgh Courier's Man from Chicago," *Western Pennsylvania History*, Fall 2014, 50.

8   Prattis, "Nonsense," 26.

9   Prattis, "Changing Years," 40.

10   Near the time that Prattis was graduated, a race riot erupted in East St. Louis, Illinois, between working-class whites and black people over housing and

jobs. Eight whites and about one hundred black people were killed in the riot. Thousands of residents fleeing the city lost their possessions and homes.

11   Prattis, "Changing Years," 42.

12   "Stand by Flag, Negroes Urged: Colored Educator Calls on Race to Do All It Can for Nation," *Detroit Free Press*, April 13, 1917, 11.

13   Prattis, "Nonsense," 43.

14   Ibid., 29.

15   Ibid.

16   Rosenberg, "Percival L. Prattis," 50.

17   Prattis, "Changing Years," 41.

18   Henry La Brie, *Perspectives of the Black Press* (Kennebunkport, ME: Mercer House Press, 1974), 67.

19   "Courier's Prattis Coming Soon; One of the Ablest Newspapermen," *The Lincoln Clarion* (Jefferson City, MO), April 12, 1946, 1.

20   "Walter White Holds Big Meetings," *Michigan State News* (Grand Rapids, MI), April 26, 1920, 1.

21   Randall Jelks, "Making Opportunity: The Struggle against Jim Crow in Grand Rapids, Michigan, 1890–1927," *Michigan Historical Review* 19, no. 2 (Fall 1993): 33.

22   Prattis, "Nonsense," 35.

23   For a thorough understanding of the life and influence of Abbott, see Ethan Michaeli, *The Defender: How the Legendary Black Newspaper Changed America: From the Age of the Pullman Porters to the Age of Obama* (Boston: Houghton Mifflin Harcourt, 2016).

24   The dispute may have involved money. Prattis was paid twenty dollars a week as city editor. He was upset to discover that a janitor in his building was earning twenty-five dollars a week.

25   To understand Barnett's commitment to Pan-Africanism and the rise and fall of the ANP, see Gerald Horne, *The Rise and Fall of the Associated Negro Press: Claude Barnett's Pan-African News and the Jim Crow Paradox* (Urbana: University of Illinois Press, 2017).

26   Vanessa K. Valdés, *Diasporic Blackness: The Life and Times of Arturo Alfonso Schomburg* (Albany: SUNY Press, 2017), 162.

27   James Logan Jenkins Jr. was another Hampton/Ferris student who worked as a writer; he was a contributor to the *Pittsburgh Courier*, focusing on the happenings in Baltimore. After Ferris, he attended Laskey Commercial College in Boston. Jenkins is one of the original founders—the "Significant Six"—of the Kappa Alpha Psi Fraternity, the Chi Chapter.

28   "Opportunity Is Now, Former Editor Says," *Pittsburgh Press*, January 10, 1975, 12.

29   Ibid.

30   For a more critical analysis, see William G. Jordan, *Black Newspapers and America's War for Democracy, 1914–1920* (Chapel Hill: University of North Carolina Press, 2003).

31   P.L. Prattis, "The Role of the Negro Press in Race Relations," transcribed speech, 1946, 2.

32   P.L. Prattis, "Significance of Segregation in Negro Journalism," transcribed speech, 2.

33   Ibid., 1.

34   Ibid., 5.

35 "Issues: Good and Bad," *Kansas Sentinel* (Topeka, Kansas), July 1, 1964, 8.

36 This publication was originally known as *Heebie Jeebies: A Sign of Intelligence*. Later, it was known as *The Light and Heebie Jeebies*, then, finally, *The Light*.

37 Johnson Publishing Company started *Jet* magazine in 1951.

38 Shelly L. Watson, "The Pittsburgh Courier: Advocate for Integration of the U.S. Armed Forces (1934–1940)" (master's thesis, San Jose State University, 2013), 26.

39 James G. Thompson, "Should I Sacrifice to Live 'Half-American'?" *Pittsburgh Courier*, January 31, 1942, 3.

40 Ibid.

41 Patrick S. Washburn, "The *Pittsburgh Courier's* Double V Campaign in 1942," *American Journalism* 3, no. 2 (1986): 73.

42 Ibid., 74.

43 This milestone was significant in United States history, but it is overshadowed by another breakthrough that year: on April 15, 1947, Jackie Robinson played in a game for the Brooklyn Dodgers, breaking a color barrier in the sport that had lasted since the 1880s. Prattis pushed Major League Baseball to sign black players more than a decade before Robinson first played for the Dodgers.

44 Rosenberg, "Percival L. Prattis," 48.

45 Ibid., 59.

46 "Black History Month, Day 3: Percival Prattis (April 27, 1895–February 29, 1980)," Nina Simone, accessed February 5, 2020, http://www.ninasimone.com/2013/02/black-history-month-percival-prattis.

47 "Ten Best: Color Lists Top Newsmen," *Pittsburgh Courier*, March 16, 1946, 3.

48 Fannie Gibson was born in Malden, West Virginia, in 1871, and graduated from Hampton Institute's normal course in 1898. She taught at Hampton until 1939, when she retired and moved to Baltimore to live with her son; see *Newport News Daily Press*, March 17, 1948, 9.

49 William I. Gibson, "A Comparative Study of the Immigrant and Negro Press in Their Relation to Social Attitudes" (master's thesis, Ohio State University, 1927), accessed February 5, 2020, etd.ohiolink.edu/pg_10?0::NO:10:P10_ACCESSION_NUM:osu1213889969.

50 "About Us," Afro: The Black Media Authority, accessed February 5, 2020, www.afro.com/about-us.

51 Carl Murphy, Wm. N. Jones, and Wm. I. Gibson, "The Afro: Seaboard's Largest Weekly," *The Crisis*, February 1938, 45.

52 Founded on the campus of Hampton Institute in 1912, the CIAA is the oldest African American athletic conference in the United States.

53 "Bill Gibson Did Much to Help," *Baltimore Afro-American*, March 5, 1963, 13.

54 An example is his report of black athletes at the 1930 Penn relays; Bill Gibson, "Hear Me Talkin' To Ya," *Baltimore Afro-American*, July 18, 1931, 12.

55 Bill Gibson, "Lefty-Loves His Right Too," *Baltimore Afro-American*, June 29, 1935, 1.

56 Gibson, "Hear Me Talkin' To Ya!" 21.

57 "S.C. Governor Raps Dewey," *Elmira (NY) Star-Gazette*, July 6, 1944, 20.

58 Olin DeWitt Talmadge Johnston served as the 98th Governor of South Carolina, 1935–1939 and 1943–1945, and represented the state in the United States Senate from 1945 until his death from pneumonia in Columbia, South Carolina, in 1965.

59 "Criticizes Dewey for Attending Gathering of Negro Editors," *Boston Globe*, July 6, 1944, 4.

Fixing More Than Teeth: African American Dentists

1   Charles A. Broaddus, from Mount Sterling, Kentucky, attended the Ferris Institute in 1923. It is unclear if he attended the Hampton Institute. Broaddus received his DDS from Temple University and operated a dental office in Trenton, New Jersey, for many years. He was a civic leader and served as the eastern vice president of the Alpha Phi Alpha organization. Indeed, Broaddus was considered one of the giants of the Alpha Phi Alpha fraternity.

2   Howard University was established in Washington, DC, by the United States Freedmen's Bureau in 1867. The Dental Department was added in 1881. In 1876, private monies were used to establish the Meharry Medical College in Nashville, Tennessee, which added a dental program in 1886. Before the Howard and Meharry dental schools were created, most black dentists were products of apprenticeships.

3   "To Feature Workers on NBC Chain Sunday: Freedom's People to Present Randolph, Famous Southnaires," *Indianapolis Recorder*, January 17, 1942, 9. The elder Dixon is not always credited with this invention.

4   Russell Dixon is pictured in Ferris Institute, *What School?* December 1920, 2.

5   Clifton O. Dummett, "American Dental Education: Contributions of Russell A. Dixon," *CDS Review*, August 1996, 28.

6   The Rosenwald Fund was established in 1917 by Julius Rosenwald and his family for "the well-being of mankind." This is similar to Woodbridge Ferris's mantra "make the world better." The Fund made fellowship grants—typically one to two thousand dollars annually—to African American artists, writers, researchers, and intellectuals from 1928 to 1948.

7   "Dr. L.H. Fairclough Protests Naming Dr. Russell Dixon as Acting Dean Howard University Dental College," *New York Age*, August 22, 1931, 5.

8   Ibid.

9   Russell A. Dixon, "Sources of Supply of Negro Health Personnel Section B: Dentists," *The Journal of Negro Education* 6, no. 3 (1937): 477–82.

10   Ibid., 482.

11   Russell A. Dixon and Grace E. Byrd, "The Supply of Negro Health Personnel-Dentists," *The Journal of Negro Education* 18, no. 3 (1949): 363.

12   *Pittsburgh Courier*, November 10, 1962, 6.

13   "Howard Dental School," *Ebony*, January 1960.

14   A child of enslaved parents, Robert Tanner Freeman was graduated from Harvard on May 18, 1869, only four years after the Civil War.

15   Harvey Webb and Lloyd Cecil Rhodes, *The Book of Presidents: Leaders of Organized Dentistry* (Charlottesville, VA: National Dental Association, 1977), 1949.

16   Ibid., 1948.

17   "'Men of Bronze' Traces Regiment's Roots," *Tampa Bay Times*, November 8, 1977, 45.

18   "Other Hampton Men at the Front," *Southern Workman*, January 1919, 45.

19   The Croix de Guerre is a French military decoration. It was first created in 1915 and consists of a square-cross medal on two crossed swords, hanging from a ribbon with various degree pins. The Croix de Guerre may either be awarded as an individual or unit award to those soldiers who distinguish themselves by acts of heroism involving combat with the enemy.

20   His thesis was titled "Study of Clinical Photography for Orthodontia Cases," and it laid the foundation for his later work as a clinician.

21   Dental ceramics are materials that are part of systems designed to produce dental prostheses used to replace missing or damaged dental structures. Ceramics are inorganic, nonmetallic materials made by heating raw minerals at high temperatures.

22   In 1921, Paxton was enrolled in the college preparatory program at Ferris. He earned his dental degree from Howard University in 1926. He served as president of the Old Dominion Dental Society in 1944.

23   "Sixty-Eight Diplomas to Institute Men," *Newport News Daily Press*, May 28, 1914, 7.

24   "Mob Uses Knife on Negro," *The Morning Tulsa Daily World*, May 2, 1921, 1.

25   "Talladega Negro Dentist Flogged: Whipped Because He Practiced among Whites, Kidnapers Tell Him," *Pensacola News Journal*, May 3, 1924, 4.

26   "Texas Negro Dentist Is Tarred and Feathered," *Alexandria (LA) Town Talk*, August 14, 1925, 1.

27   "Testimony in Murder Trial Now Underway," *Kingsport (TN) News*, March 30, 1951, 20.

28   "Ex-Hampton Resident Dies After Assault," *Newport News Daily Press*, February 8, 1951, 5.

29   "Dentist Slain," *Pittsburgh Courier*, February 17, 1951, 1.

30   "Beaten to Death by 2 Whites," *Pittsburgh Courier*, February 17, 1951, 1.

31   "Find 2 Youths Guilty in Death of Santa Cruz," *Newport News Daily Press*, July 1, 1951, 2.

Last Words

1   The Fairman Building is directly across the street from the Northern Bank Building, which Mr. Ferris rented to serve as classrooms for the early Ferris Industrial School (the building is now home to a Fifth Third Bank and is known as the first permanent site of the Ferris school).

2   "History," Old Settlers Reunion.com, accessed February 5, 2020, www.oldsettlersreunion.com/index.php/history.

3   "Michigan's 83 Counties: Mecosta," *Michigan History Magazine*, March–April 1987, 15–17.

4   The Ferris State University campus is thirty-one miles from Idlewild and thirty-three miles from Baldwin.

5   1914 Ferris Calendar, Ferris Archives, no publication information.

6   We also discovered a minstrel show on campus in 1928, see Joseph E. Deupree, *A Century of Opportunity: A Centennial History of Ferris State College* (Big Rapids, MI: J.E. Deupree, 1982), 184.

7   Gerrit Masselink came to Ferris Institute in June 1898, where he remained until his death in 1929, with the exception of one year when he held a position as an instructor at MAC.

8   "Teachers' Institute," *Owosso (MI) Times*, January 19, 1917, 1.

9   Roger L. Rosentreter, *Michigan: A History of Explorers, Entrepreneurs, and Everyday People* (Ann Arbor: University of Michigan Press, 2014), 263.

10   James A. Henretta, David Brody, and Lynn Dumenil, *America's History, Volume Two: Since 1865* (Boston: Bedford/St. Martin's, 2008), 681.

11   McLeod's was the only class to graduate from Fort Des Moines. The War Department closed it soon after their departure. Future black candidates attended either special training camps in Puerto Rico, the Philippines, Hawaii, and Panama or regular officer training facilities in the United States.

12   The cadet class included: Elder Watson Diggs, who cofounded Kappa Alpha Psi Fraternity in 1911; Frank Coleman and Edgar Love, who cofounded Omega Psi Phi Fraternity the same year; Samuel Joe Brown, Charles Howard, and James Morris, who founded the National Bar Association in 1925; Charles Hamilton Houston, a Harvard-educated attorney known as "the man who killed Jim Crow."

13   Charles Johnson Jr., *African Americans and ROTC: Military, Naval, and Aeroscience Programs at Historically Black Colleges, 1916–1973* (Jefferson, NC: McFarland and Co., 2002), 52.

14   Ibid., 33.

15   "Annual Report of the Principal," *Southern Workman*, June 1921, 261–62.

16   Little is known about McLeod's time at Ferris Institute. We do know that he is listed in the Institute's Catalog for 1922–1923, though that publication showed students from September 6, 1920, to February 10, 1922.

17   *Crimson and Gold*, 1920, 102.

18   We were unable to definitively identify him in the ROTC photographs, but we were able to locate a photograph of him from his time at Hampton.

19   Samuel A. Barnes, "Signaling Souls on the Western Front," *The Army Communicator*, 1980, 31.

20   Ibid., 33.

21   After he was graduated, Bouldin operated a dental practice in Peoria, Illinois. He died in 1952.

22   After graduating from Hampton in 1912, he attended the Ferris Institute in 1914 as a carpentry student. The only other information I have about Lipscomb is that in 1942 he lived in Philadelphia, Pennsylvania, and worked for the United States Post Office. The National Archives at St. Louis; St. Louis, Missouri; *World War II Draft Cards (Fourth Registration) for the State of Pennsylvania*; Record Group Title: *Records of the Selective Service System, 1926–1975*; Record Group Number: *147*; Series Number: *M1951*.

23   William Garrett Hearn studied bricklaying at Hampton, 1911–1914, and college preparatory at Ferris, 1920–1922. He appeared in the 1921 Ferris Institute yearbook. Hearn is listed as a resident of Montréal, Québec. The Clarke brothers were also listed as being from Canada.

24   Letter from Paul Maurice Floyd to Miss Myrilla J. Sherman, Hampton Registrar, March 5, 1922.

25   "Graduates and Ex-Students," *Southern Workman*, February 1918, 109. Lowe is shown in the 1917 Ferris yearbook with two groups: bookkeepers and bankers. He registered for the World War I draft while living and working in Grand Rapids.

26   "Graduates and Ex-Students," *Southern Workman*, 1924, 90.

27   Gerald White, "Under Scholarship: 50-Year-Old Trust Fund to Be Used for Helping Worthy Negro Students," *The Cincinnati Enquirer*, March 14, 1964, 11.

28   "A Survey of Historic Architecture in Dinwiddie County, Virginia," Virginia Department of Historic Resources, Richmond, Autumn 2009–Spring 2010, 109, accessed February 5, 2020, www.dhr.virginia.gov/pdf_files/SpecialCollections/ DW-099_Survey_AE_Dinwiddie_County_2010_3NorthArchitects_Report.pdf.

29   "Phelps-Stokes Fund records," New York Public Library: Archives and Manuscripts, accessed February 5, 2020, http://archives.nypl.org/scm/20936.

30   Roy was a carpentry student at Hampton and was graduated in 1911. After Hampton, he became a carpentry instructor at Florida Agricultural and Mechanical College in Tallahassee. Seeking a career change, Roy enrolled at the Ferris Institute in the Commercial Department in 1913.

31   It is unclear if Barlow attended the Hampton Institute.

32   Victor Hugo Green, *The Negro Motorist Green Book* (Harlem, NY: self-published, 1936–1966).

33   Reginald Shareef, *The Roanoke Valley's African American Heritage* (Virginia Beach: Donning Company Publishers, 1996), 148.

34   Hazel Bass was from Boyne City, Michigan. She was enrolled in the Shorthand Department. The caption accompanying her yearbook picture read, "Like a bee she works all the day"; *Crimson and Gold*, 1924, 57.

35   Edith Wolter, "Dear Governor Ferris," Michigan History, 1958, 378.

36   Ibid.

37   Ibid., 379.

38   *Catalog of Ferris Institute, 1917–1918*, 69; *Catalog of Ferris Institute, 1920–1921*, 134.

39   During this time, Hampton men like Gideon Smith, Bishop Brown, James Duncan, William Howard, and others also attended Ferris Institute.

40   "Local Woman Does It: Underground Railroad Story Finally Compiled," *Lansing State Journal*, November 14, 1960, 11.

41   "Blanche B. Coggan Papers," Charles H. Wright Museum of African American History, 4, accessed February 5, docplayer.net/100416561-Blanche-b-coggan-papers-mss173.html.

42   "Champion of Blacks, Indians Sees Flaws in Bicentennial," *Lansing State Journal*, April 30, 1975, 43.

43   Ibid.

Index

Page numbers in *italic* refer to illustrations. "Passim" (literally "scattered") indicates intermittent discussion of a topic over a cluster of pages.

About the Authors

David Pilgrim is a public speaker and one of America's leading experts on issues relating to multiculturalism, diversity, and race relations. An applied sociologist, he is best known as the founder and director of the Jim Crow Museum: a 14,000+ collection of racist artifacts located at Ferris State University. Pilgrim is also the vice president of Diversity, Inclusion, and Strategic Initiatives for the university. He is the author of *Understanding Jim Crow* and *Watermelons, Nooses, and Straight Razors*.

Franklin Hughes is a multimedia specialist at Ferris State University. He has created numerous videos, graphics, and web materials for the world-renowned Jim Crow Museum and other Ferris entities. However, Franklin has not restricted himself to multimedia projects. He has also dabbled in writing, conducted research, and become an adept public presenter. Franklin has had an interesting and varied professional career, having worked in loss prevention, corrections, civilian Air Force Security Forces, sports video, and television production. Franklin is married, with five grown children he enjoys spending time with, camping, traveling, and serving at church.

David Eisler has served as president of Ferris State University since July 2003. He believes that higher education should prepare students for successful careers, create a pattern of intellectual rigor, develop a commitment to community engagement, and provide the foundation for lifelong learning.

ABOUT PM PRESS

PM Press is an independent, radical publisher of books and media to educate, entertain, and inspire. Founded in 2007 by a small group of people with decades of publishing, media, and organizing experience, PM Press amplifies the voices of radical authors, artists, and activists. Our aim is to deliver bold political ideas and vital stories to all walks of life and arm the dreamers to demand the impossible. We have sold millions of copies of our books, most often one at a time, face to face. We're old enough to know what we're doing and young enough to know what's at stake. Join us to create a better world.

PM Press
PO Box 23912
Oakland, CA 94623
www.pmpress.org

PM Press in Europe
europe@pmpress.org
www.pmpress.org.uk

FRIENDS OF PM PRESS

These are indisputably momentous times—the financial system is melting down globally and the Empire is stumbling. Now more than ever there is a vital need for radical ideas.

In the years since its founding—and on a mere shoestring—PM Press has risen to the formidable challenge of publishing and distributing knowledge and entertainment for the struggles ahead. With over 450 releases to date, we have published an impressive and stimulating array of literature, art, music, politics, and culture. Using every available medium, we've succeeded in connecting those hungry for ideas and information to those putting them into practice.

Friends of PM allows you to directly help impact, amplify, and revitalize the discourse and actions of radical writers, filmmakers, and artists. It provides us with a stable foundation from which we can build upon our early successes and provides a much-needed subsidy for the materials that can't necessarily pay their own way. You can help make that happen—and receive every new title automatically delivered to your door once a month—by joining as a Friend of PM Press. And, we'll throw in a free T-shirt when you sign up.

Here are your options:

- **$30 a month** Get all books and pamphlets plus 50% discount on all webstore purchases

- **$40 a month** Get all PM Press releases (including CDs and DVDs) plus 50% discount on all webstore purchases

- **$100 a month** Superstar—Everything plus PM merchandise, free downloads, and 50% discount on all webstore purchases

For those who can't afford $30 or more a month, we have **Sustainer Rates** at $15, $10 and $5. Sustainers get a free PM Press T-shirt and a 50% discount on all purchases from our website.

Your Visa or Mastercard will be billed once a month, until you tell us to stop. Or until our efforts succeed in bringing the revolution around. Or the financial meltdown of Capital makes plastic redundant. Whichever comes first.

Understanding Jim Crow: Using Racist Memorabilia to Teach Tolerance and Promote Social Justice

David Pilgrim with a foreword by
Henry Louis Gates Jr.

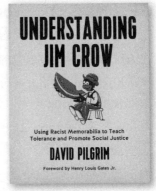

ISBN: 978-1-62963-114-1
$24.95   208 pages

For many people, especially those who came of age after landmark civil rights legislation was passed, it is difficult to understand what it was like to be an African American living under Jim Crow segregation in the United States. Most young Americans have little or no knowledge about restrictive covenants, literacy tests, poll taxes, lynchings, and other oppressive features of the Jim Crow racial hierarchy. Even those who have some familiarity with the period may initially view racist segregation and injustices as mere relics of a distant, shameful past. A a proper understanding of race relations in this country must include a solid knowledge of Jim Crow—how it emerged, what it was like, how it ended, and its impact on the culture.

Understanding Jim Crow introduces readers to the Jim Crow Museum of Racist Memorabilia, a collection of more than ten thousand contemptible collectibles that are used to engage visitors in intense and intelligent discussions about race, race relations, and racism. The items are offensive. They were meant to be offensive. The items in the Jim Crow Museum served to dehumanize blacks and legitimized patterns of prejudice, discrimination, and segregation.

Using racist objects as teaching tools seems counterintuitive—and, quite frankly, needlessly risky. Many Americans are already apprehensive discussing race relations, especially in settings where their ideas are challenged. The museum and this book exist to help overcome our collective trepidation and reluctance to talk about race.

Fully illustrated, and with context provided by the museum's founder and director David Pilgrim, *Understanding Jim Crow* is both a grisly tour through America's past and an auspicious starting point for racial understanding and healing.

"One of the most important contributions to the study of American history that I have ever experienced."
—Henry Louis Gates Jr., director of the W.E.B. Du Bois Institute for African American Research

Watermelons, Nooses, and Straight Razors: Stories from the Jim Crow Museum

Author: David Pilgrim with a Foreword by Debby Irving

ISBN: 978-1-62963-437-1
$24.95   272 pages

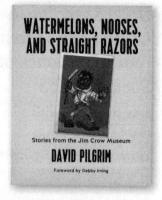

All groups tell stories, but some groups have the power to impose their stories on others, to label others, stigmatize others, paint others as undesirables—and to have these stories presented as scientific fact, God's will, or wholesome entertainment. *Watermelons, Nooses, and Straight Razors* examines the origins and significance of several longstanding antiblack stories and the caricatures and stereotypes that support them. Here readers will find representations of the lazy, childlike Sambo, the watermelon-obsessed pickaninny, the buffoonish minstrel, the subhuman savage, the loyal and contented mammy and Tom, and the menacing, razor-toting coon and brute.

Malcolm X and James Baldwin both refused to eat watermelon in front of white people. They were aware of the jokes and other stories about African Americans stealing watermelons, fighting over watermelons, even being transformed into watermelons. Did racial stories influence the actions of white fraternities and sororities who dressed in blackface and mocked black culture, or employees who hung nooses in their workplaces? What stories did the people who refer to Serena Williams and other dark-skinned athletes as apes or baboons hear? Is it possible that a white South Carolina police officer who shot a fleeing black man had never heard stories about scary black men with straight razors or other weapons? Antiblack stories still matter.

Watermelons, Nooses, and Straight Razors uses images from the Jim Crow Museum, the nation's largest publicly accessible collection of racist objects. These images are evidence of the social injustice that Martin Luther King Jr. referred to as "a boil that can never be cured so long as it is covered up but must be exposed to the light of human conscience and the air of national opinion before it can be cured." Each chapter concludes with a story from the author's journey, challenging the integrity of racial narratives.

"Pilgrim's book is a well-researched, comprehensive, and ever-present documentation of where we've been and where we still are. All of America needs to confront these injustices in order to put them where they belong, in the past, not the present."
—Philip J. Merrill, CEO and founder of Nanny Jack & Co.

CIVIO: A Civil Rights Strategy Card Game

Reach And Teach illustrated
by Innosanto Nagara

ISBN: 978-1-60486-344-4
$14.95

CIVIO is a strategy card game that explores the relationship of issues, freedoms, laws, and Supreme Court cases that have both strengthened and reduced civil rights and civil liberties.

Using a handful of cards representing laws, Supreme Court decisions, constitutional amendments, key issues, and freedoms, you are in a race against other players to combine these cards into precedents. The more points you earn, the higher your ranking. In time, you could become Chief Justice of the Supreme Court!

CIVIO comes with a deck of 78 cards, each beautifully and uniquely illustrated, four blank case cards for customizing the game, and instruction booklets for playing two versions of the game. The game is manufactured and assembled by a worker-owned (and union-labor) cooperative using recycled paper and soy-based ink.

CIVIO was created by the award-winning team at Reach And Teach and illustrated by bestselling author/illustrator Innosanto Nagara (*A Is for Activist*).

(H)afrocentric Comics: Volumes 1-4

Juliana "Jewels" Smith, illustrated by Ronald Nelson, with colors/lettering by Mike Hampton, and a foreword by Kiese Laymon

ISBN: 978-1-62963-448-7
$20.00   136 pages

Glyph Award winner Juliana "Jewels" Smith and illustrator Ronald Nelson have created an unflinching visual and literary tour-de-force on the most pressing issues of the day— including gentrification, police violence, and the housing crisis—with humor and biting satire. *(H)afrocentric* tackles racism, patriarchy, and popular culture head-on. Unapologetic and unabashed, *(H)afrocentric* introduces us to strong yet vulnerable students of color, as well as an aesthetic that connects current Black pop culture to an organic reappropriation of hip hop fashion circa the early 90s.

We start the journey when gentrification strikes the neighborhood surrounding Ronald Reagan University. Naima Pepper recruits a group of disgruntled undergrads of color to combat the onslaught by creating and launching the first and only anti-gentrification social networking site, mydiaspora.com. The motley crew is poised to fight back against expensive avocado toast, muted Prius cars, exorbitant rent, and cultural appropriation. Whether Naima and the gang are transforming social media, leading protests, fighting rent hikes, or working as "Racial Translators," the students at Ronald Reagan University take movements to a new level by combining their tech-savvy, Black Millennial sensibilities with their individual backgrounds, goals, and aspirations.

"Smith's comics ooze with originality."
—AFROPUNK

"(H)afrocentric is a book that is incredibly contemporary and fits the progressive minds of today's readers. It tackles issues of intersectionality and gentrification in ways that are not only informative but also entertaining. It's unlike any comic book I've ever read."
—Jamie Broadnax, founder and managing editor of Blackgirlnerds.com

"(H)afrocentric is fully dope, artistic, brilliantly drawn, styled, and wonderfully radical with an awesomely fiery heroine! Juliana Smith and her team are to be commended for this desperately needed political and cultural contribution. Get into it and grab your soapboxes!"
—Jared A. Ball, author of *I Mix What I Like! A Mixtape Manifesto*

Look for Me in the Whirlwind: From the Panther 21 to 21st-Century Revolutions

Sekou Odinga, Dhoruba Bin Wahad, Jamal Joseph
Edited by Matt Meyer & déqui kioni-sadiki
with a Foreword by Imam Jamil Al-Amin, and an Afterword by Mumia Abu-Jamal

ISBN: 978-1-62963-389-3
$26.95   648 pages

Amid music festivals and moon landings, the tumultuous year of 1969 included an infamous case in the annals of criminal justice and Black liberation: the New York City Black Panther 21. Though some among the group had hardly even met one another, the 21 were rounded up by the FBI and New York Police Department in an attempt to disrupt and destroy the organization that was attracting young people around the world. Involving charges of conspiracy to commit violent acts, the Panther 21 trial—the longest and most expensive in New York history—revealed the illegal government activities which led to exile, imprisonment on false charges, and assassination of Black liberation leaders. Solidarity for the 21 also extended well beyond "movement" circles and included mainstream publication of their collective autobiography, *Look for Me in the Whirlwind*, which is reprinted here for the first time.

Look for Me in the Whirlwind: From the Panther 21 to 21st-Century Revolutions contains the entire original manuscript, and includes new commentary from surviving members of the 21: Sekou Odinga, Dhoruba Bin Wahad, Jamal Joseph, and Shaba Om. Still-imprisoned Sundiata Acoli, Imam Jamil Al-Amin, and Mumia Abu-Jamal contribute new essays. Never or rarely seen poetry and prose from Afeni Shakur, Kuwasi Balagoon, Ali Bey Hassan, and Michael "Cetewayo" Tabor is included. Early Panther leader and jazz master Bilal Sunni-Ali adds a historical essay and lyrics from his composition "Look for Me in the Whirlwind," and coeditors kioni-sadiki, Meyer, and Panther rank-and-file member Cyril "Bullwhip" Innis Jr. help bring the story up to date.

At a moment when the Movement for Black Lives recites the affirmation that "it is our duty to win," penned by Black Liberation Army (BLA) militant Assata Shakur, those who made up the BLA and worked alongside of Assata are largely unknown. This book—with archival photos from David Fenton, Stephen Shames, and the private collections of the authors— provides essential parts of a hidden and missing-in-action history. Going well beyond the familiar and mythologized nostalgic Panther narrative, *From the Panther 21 to 21st-Century Revolutions* explains how and why the Panther legacy is still relevant and vital today.

Up a Creek, with a Paddle:
Tales of Canoeing and Life

James W. Loewen

ISBN: 978-1-62963-827-0
$15.95   176 pages

Up a Creek, with a Paddle is an intimate and often
humorous memoir by the author of Lies My Teacher Told
Me, James W. Loewen, who holds the distinction of being
the best-selling living sociologist today. Rivers are good
metaphors for life, and paddling for living. In this little
book, Loewen skillfully makes these connections without sermonizing, resulting in
nuggets of wisdom about how to live, how to act meaningfully, and perhaps how
to die. Loewen also returns to his life's work and gently addresses the origins of
racism and inequality, the theory of history, confronting institutional dishonesty,
but mostly, as in his life, he finds rueful humor in every canoeing fiasco—and he
has had many!

Amid the laughter and often self-deprecating humility, Loewen weaves together
deep and important sociological ideas that penetrate the core of our social world,
revealing why and how the world is marred by injustice and inequality.

"The incomparable Jim Loewen has written a memoir like no other. I laughed at his
delightful stories of canoeing fiascos that repeatedly answered his question, 'What
could possibly go wrong?' In quieter intervals, I learned from his reflections on history,
ethics, and race relations. About death he is funny—'I'm not dead yet but I'm working
on it'—but unflinching. His spirit will live on, though, in the ways that history is told.
This book's energy can sustain and inspire those who follow."
—Peggy McIntosh, author of White Privilege: Unpacking the Invisible Knapsack

"He is the high school history teacher we all should have had."
—Carol Kammen, author of On Doing Local History

"Loewen is a one-man historical truth squad. . . . He has written a devastating portrait of
how American history is commemorated."
—The Nation

"Loewen himself is forever young at heart: energetic, curious, skeptical, irreverent, and
yet deeply idealistic."
—James Goodman, professor of history at Rutgers University, Newark, and Pulitzer
Prize finalist